Three Poisons

greed – ill will – delusion

Kriben Pillay

NON-DUALITY PRESS

THREE POISONS

First edition November 2014 by NON-DUALITY PRESS
© Kriben Pillay 2014
© Non-Duality Press 2014

NON-DUALITY PRESS | PO Box 2228 | Salisbury | SP2 2GZ
United Kingdom

ISBN: 978-1-908664-51-8

www.non-dualitypress.org

... when we penetrate to the roots of the problems they analyse, in each case we end up uncovering greed, ill will and delusion – 'the three poisons'...

David R. Loy author of *The World Is Made of Stories*

Table of Contents

Acknowledgements • vii

Foreword • xi

An Unethical Clearance • 1

The Twofold Tamil Rule • 21

Imagining John Lennon • 91

Acknowledgements

This collection of short stories was inspired by the writings of the Buddhist scholar, David Loy, which first brought to my attention the concept of the 'three poisons' – greed, ill will and delusion. After some time I realised that I had written stories that speak to each of these poisons: 'Imagining John Lennon'[1] (delusion) was written in early 2006, and 'The Twofold Tamil Rule' (ill will) in the latter half of the same year. 'An Unethical Clearance' (greed) was written in 2010. While each story foregrounds a particular poison, the other poisons, as in life, are also present because they are all interconnected.

The story of the Twofold Tamil Rule could not have happened without my brother Indiren, who co-formulated the actual rule some thirty-three years ago. And I am thankful to my mother, Daya, my late father, Reg, and his late sister, Janey, whose family stories inspired the telling of this tale, where

1. It appears in *The Vintage Book of South African Indian Writing* (2010), edited by Rajendra Chetty.

some details, characters and situations are taken from the histories of both my maternal and paternal families and have been re-created to serve the truth of this narrative.

A special thank you to historian Dr Keith Tankard for patiently answering all my questions. I found his website (www.knowledge4africa.com) a wonderful source of previously unknown information about the place of my birth.

Likewise, I was graciously assisted with archival records by Nasreen Salig of the Durban Cultural and Documentation Centre.

Gracious thanks go to my hosts in India, T.K. Rangarajan and Mohan and Girija Nair, who, on different occasions, took me through the areas of my ancestors in South India, which inspired the setting of the Indian segment. They were wonderful founts of information about local cultures.

I am also indebted to the Wikipedia internet website for valuable background information.

Thanks to my many friends who listened to me as the story took shape, especially my dear friend Shirley Bell. And later, Rajendra Chetty and Fiona Farquharson, who gave invaluable editorial input.

To my family I am always thankful for giving me the time and space to write; to my son Kialan, for stretching the storyteller in me; to my daughter Siddharthiya, for listening to my 'voices' as characters defined themselves; and to my wife Uma for her love and unconditional support.

And finally, my gratitude to the National Arts Council of South Africa for the grant to write the *Twofold Tamil Rule* novella.

Foreword

Kriben Pillay's writing endeavours are as remarkable as they are versatile, as evidenced by this collection of short stories: 'An Unethical Clearance', 'The Twofold Tamil Rule' and 'Imagining John Lennon'.

'An Unethical Clearance' is an accomplished piece where Pillay transcribes the adversary of clumsy bureaucracy to the new South Africa. His literary form here is taut and precisely controlled. The subtly-controlled and admirably-contrived episodes of comedy reach waves of climactic laughability. At first Shakespeare is black, as he may be derived from the legendary Zulu King Shaka's spear and then just as easily he may be Muslim, from Shaik's spear. Pillay thrusts quite sharply at the pomposity of academe as well as the government machinery that collaborates in the great mill of unlearning. At the heart of the tale, again, in the midst of the seemingly light and airy matter of his satire, there is the twist whereby 'unethical clearance' applies to the admission of harmful baby food as much as it does to the ethical suitability of a candidate for research. All the bricks and plaster of the edifice of 'government' come tumbling down upon this explosion of the inequity and iniquity of conditions in the new South Africa which perpetrates the same blunders as the old; if not worse, given that the new promised so much better.

'The Twofold Tamil Rule' is the kernel of a much longer history of the lives of Indians who made South Africa their home. The novella, bordering on epic proportions, traces three generations of the Pillai family. The author does not dwell on the hardship and deprivation of those who ultimately succeeded so well in the country. There is a light, humorous touch to his narration that beguiles the darker strands of the political subtext. In many ways, this reflects the perceptive coping mechanisms of immigrants who were exploited considerably more than they were welcomed. Self-effacement, resourcefulness, hard work and an intuitive genius are both the material of the fiction as well as the stuff of the actual lives of the author's family. In this regard, Pillay's work accords with the axes of so much diaspora writing: his fictional constructs are also outlines of profoundly personal memories. The annals of his family and the boundaries of formal autobiography are blurred by pain and suffering into biography and larger commu-nity history. Reading these creative writing pieces is therefore at first engaging and instantly amusing, but this surface superficiality is the narrative lure to a potent exemplification of inequality and abuse. So

Pillay's playful play on words and consistent love of word-play is itself a metaphor for the surreal mystifications of 'ordinary life' as it exists for those privileged to enjoy it. For himself and his fictional representatives or representations, the ordinary kindnesses of 'ordinary life' dissolve beneath them. 'You stupid superstitious coolie' is the denigration that 'common' inhabitants of the colonial establishment were free to hurl at the 'other' without legal restraint or consequence.

Life in this shadow-land of semi-recognition is portrayed without malice. 'The Twofold Tamil Rule' incorporates this unhateful voice to speak of hatred and prejudice. In so doing, the narrator succeeds in architecting a convincing fictional structure that resonates with the depth and height of both plain living and high thinking. The boundaries of intellectual and moral substance are deftly galvanized to the solid experience of daily existence. The overtly comic detail of such incidents as the aubergine over the head is saved from slapstick by the inwardly reflected justice of Pillay's own integrity. He is ever vigilant and protective of his and his people's worth. Healthy iconoclasm runs through so many of the incidents of this quick-moving history of a family: they overcome impossible obstacles with easy commonsense and a complete disregard for the humbug of colonial administration. Despite all the legal outrages inflicted on the Pillai dynasty, there is so little indignation in return. The word 'coolie' may be thrown, but the reply in narrative politeness and real-life success is not only the silence of happy living, but the mark of cultured beings. After all, Tamil remains one of the longest surviving classical languages and its literature is described as one of the great classical traditions of the world.

In 'Imagining John Lennon', Pillay astutely and creatively interprets the rapidly changing tenor of our times and turns this into the absorbing stuff of fiction. The story bears testament to the subtlety of Pillay's understanding of philosophy, the slippery cleft between normality/madness and the complexity of ordinary lives in an extraordinary society. This is the vision of an insightful and nuanced writer.

Professor Rajendra Chetty
Cape Town

greed

An Unethical Clearance

When the phone rang, Lucky moved in one fluid athletic arc from sleeping in bed to sitting in a chair facing his desk and reaching for his cell phone placed next to his laptop; a choreographer's delight in his display of grace and acute physical presence. More so, because Lucky was blind.

'Hello,' said Lucky, in a voice deeply mature beyond his years, fresh in its rich bass tones, showing no signs of recent sleep.

'Is that Mr Zulu?' enquired the female voice on the other side.

'Yes,' replied Lucky, 'this is Lucky Zulu speaking. How can I help you?'

'Mr Zulu,' came the reply, 'I am the postgraduate Faculty Administrator at the university, and I am afraid I have some bad news about your graduation.'

'What kind of bad news?' asked Lucky anxiously, as his mind quickly surveyed the processes that he had engaged in to comply with the examination of his doctoral thesis in English literature.

The thesis was formatted according to the faculty guidelines. One point five line spacing in Times New Roman at 11 points. Check.

The front pages had Roman numerals while the study itself had ordinary numbers. Check.

All citations had page numbers and references were formatted according to the Harvard referencing system. Check.

He had submitted his Intention to Submit form to the faculty office six months before submitting his thesis for examination. Check.

The four spiral-bound examination copies were accompanied by a plagiarism report. Check.

Permission to submit for examination was approved by his supervisor. Check.

All corrections contained in the three examiner's reports were attended to and signed off by his supervisor. Check.

The required number of final version hardbound copies were submitted timeously. Check.

'Then what is the problem?' thought Lucky as he waited to hear the bad news.

'We've only just discovered that you don't have ethical clearance,' said the voice firmly, 'and because of this we cannot include your name in the graduation programme for this year which, as you know, is next week.'

'There must be some kind of mistake,' replied Lucky, who knew of ethical clearances from his friends. The objective of ethical clearance was to ensure ethical conduct on the part of the researcher towards the researched, be they animal or human subjects. The notion of ethical research gained momentum when it was discovered just how unethical some of the research conducted by universities and research institutions had been, especially in the field of drug research where research subjects – taken from marginalised, destitute communities, in exchange for very little money – were used as guinea pigs in the quest to find the latest cures for old and new diseases. Soon the notion extended to the social sciences where it was argued, and rightfully so, that participants in a research study were also potentially vulnerable and needed some kind of legal protection in the event of a researcher behaving unethically.

'My thesis is on Shakespeare, and it involved no live humans, only some dead ones and lots of reading and writing,' said Lucky.

'I'm afraid that doesn't matter,' said the Faculty Administrator, a faint hint of righteousness edging her voice as she explained further. 'As of this year, all research in the faculty requires ethical clearance, it's a requirement of the Ministry of Health.'

'The Ministry of Health?' queried Lucky incredulously. 'What do they have to do with literature, especially Shakespeare?'

'The Ministry of Health,' replied the Administrator, getting into her stride, 'has passed legislation, which says that all studies that involve human subjects, dead or otherwise, must have ethical clearances. Our university has to comply. You cannot graduate without an ethical clearance number.'

'But my supervisor…' began Lucky, but before he could complete his sentence, the Administrator continued.

'Yes, your supervisor was wrong in not informing you of this necessary process, and he has been reprimanded for this, but the fact remains, you don't have ethical clearance, but there is a way out. We are willing to work with you on this.'

'And that is?' asked Lucky, who was beginning to feel like a man trapped in a maze in the dark.

'You can apply for retrospective clearance provided you fill in the detailed ten-page application form, which will then serve before the faculty ethical clearance committee, before going for final approval to the university-wide ethics board. The whole process takes about six weeks. But because graduation is next week, realistically we can only take the process forward for next year's graduation.'

'Six weeks!' exclaimed Lucky. 'This is ridiculous. I am coming over to see the Dean.'

'Yes, I understand your situation Mr Zulu, but as a university we have to comply with government regulations, or else as an institution we face severe consequences, like having our degrees withdrawn, or worse still, losing our subsidies,' said the Dean in his slow, measured way, which made Lucky feel that he didn't understand.

'How could he?' thought Lucky, as the Dean rambled on inanely about the need for the country to benchmark itself against what was happening in first world countries. And how they were doing Lucky a favour by granting him a retrospective clearance, when, in fact, that was somewhat illogical (as the Dean pointed out logically), since the research had already been completed. And hence the need to follow procedure to the letter, in case there was a government audit.

'More of your conversation would infect my brain,' thought Lucky. 'How could I even consider him opposing an idiotic system when he is so much in its debt?' was Lucky's next thought. Lucky was mindful of the layered implications of this thought, especially its lack of political correctness.

'What the hell,' said Lucky to himself, 'my thesis is both politically correct and incorrect; it's simply a matter of how you're looking at it.'

Indeed, Lucky's intellectual labour of three years was highly novel. With breathtaking creative scholarship, Lucky set out to prove that Shakespeare was African. Not just African because of themes which resonate with the African mind, but literally African. Hence the title: Shaik Peer, Shakespeare and Shaka's Spear.

In a leap of linguistic licence, Lucky argued, with meticulous attention to scholarly detail, that the honorific title *Shaik*, which was accorded to Arabic tribal elders and great Islamic scholars, was the root of the name *Shaka*, the leader who unified the Zulu people. And in a wheel of transforming connections, Shaik Peer was actually the real Shakespeare; the name of the former travelling with nomadic tribes from Northern Africa to the furthest south, to take root finally in the heroic leader Shaka, the founder of a nation. Lucky found a curious bit of historical synchronicity: Shaik Peer was a writer and linguist of unsurpassed genius, and he not only intimated his real identity in the name of a relatively unknown rural English actor, but was also part of an international Brotherhood of Intellectuals across religions, whose patron was the great Greek goddess Athena, the 'Shaker of Spears'. This synchronicity, more than two centuries after Shaik Peer's time, was to come full continental circle; his name arising in the great Zulu leader with a spear. Shaka's Spear. Such was Lucky's thesis: The Dark Lady of the sonnets was not a mystery; she was African. And so was the writer.

For Lucky, his theory was just as probable as all the other constructed ones.

'Everything is connected,' Lucky would always say. But how it was connected to not having ethical clearance, he could not answer. So he stood up, deftly placing his hand on the shoulder of the pretty volunteer who assisted him as a disabled student, and said:

'Professor, this is not right, and just how I found out that Shakespeare is not who we think he is, so

I am going to find out what is going on with these ethical clearances. In my case, this serves no one, but is simply frustrating. This is an administrative decision on the university's part, imposed perhaps by the Act passed by the Ministry of Health, so it can be challenged in court. Any such decision can. We can't be led by those who claim to see, but who are actually blind. I must do this, because nothing will come of nothing.'

In that moment, Lucky dimly began to see some kind of connection, but what it was precisely, he was not certain.

❧

Lucky had always been a popular student among his peers. Graced with exceedingly good looks, he had no shortage of female volunteers to escort him around the university campus, and having endured his disability all his life, he became quite adept at all things technological, especially electronic communications.

With the aid of Facebook, Lucky mobilised hundreds of his fellow students within a few hours.

'Hi guys, I'm having a problem with my faculty; they say I cannot graduate next week. I need your help,' was the brief message that went out on the social network.

The next day the university community was greeted by placard-bearing students with signs which read:

Don't interfere
With Shakespeare

And:

If Lucky doesn't graduate
Then see and hear
We're going to shake
Shaka's spear

The Principal of the university was alarmed by the student action, particularly as she had no idea what it was all about. The Dean was called in, who simply said that his faculty was following university procedures.

'The university Research Office has to comply with government regulations concerning all research and ethical processes. Our hands are tied,' said the Dean deferentially.

'But surely, given the nature of this particular study, we can speed up the process,' stated the Principal, as she became aware of the growing sound of the students chanting 'Don't interfere with Shakespeare. Don't interfere with Shakespeare. Don't…'

'Unfortunately, to comply with the Ministry of Health process, we have implemented an electronic system that ensures that all ethical clearance applications go through the various approving structures in an orderly fashion, and this ensures that we have an audit trail to comply with the Act. We cannot undo the system because it is being monitored by the central system housed in the Ministry of Health, and it automatically prevents any illegal entries. However, the real issue is that Mr Zulu does not want to apply for ethical clearance; he says it's unethical.'

As the Dean said this, he was wistfully reminded of his deep concern about this matter; one less graduating doctoral student for the current academic cycle, which in turn impacted on his performance management agreement. And a substantially decreased subsidy for the faculty. This was not his lucky day. Within himself he felt something stirring... Yes! He found that he wanted Lucky Zulu to graduate; he, too, wanted to join the students and chant, 'Don't interfere with Shakespeare.'

'I must do something, or this will turn ugly for us,' said the Principal, her words shaking the Dean out of his self-pitying reverie. 'I know the Minister of Health personally. We were in the struggle together. I will give her a call now.'

The Minister of Health was nonplussed about the whole affair.

'Ethical what?' she asked more than once. And when the details were eventually communicated, she replied, 'This falls under the Director of Health. As you were speaking I was looking at his performance agreement, and I see that "effecting a national regulatory mechanism for ethics and research at all tertiary institutions" is one of his key performance areas. But what has this got to do with Shakespeare?'

∂

The Director of Health was not in the best of moods when the Minister phoned him and questioned him on the matter. A looming crisis in the Ministry was consuming his attention, and although irritated by the Minister's call, he was not blind to the fact that he was politically obliged to entertain the Minister's query.

'I will have to look into it, Minister, because, as you know, we created a special committee to draft the policy that finally became an Act of Parliament. This committee was made up of highly esteemed specialists in ethics and research. And we used a qualified consulting firm to drive the process. The fact that it was accepted by parliament tells us that we did our work.'

What the Director omitted to tell the Minister was that the qualified consultancy firm was made up of some family members and friends who had hastily formed a company when the contract was put out to tender. The Director's presence in the tendering process insured that they were awarded the tender. In turn the company hired a junior social science researcher – because she came cheap – to lead the team that would knock the policy into shape. And at first they couldn't. The specialists all nit-picked on the details of the policy, what to leave in and what to exclude, and the junior researcher floundered in the depths of jargon. The budget was running out as more meetings were required to continue the work of the committee, and the consulting firm, fearing that their substantially large profits would be eaten into by bickering academics unable to arrive at a consensus, eventually approached the Director for a resolution to the matter. After all, his share of the profits would also be affected.

'It's simple,' he said, looking at what the committee had already arrived at. 'We'll just include the generic term "social processes" to cover any areas not covered by the other terms, and in this way no form of research that may raise ethical issues will escape the net.'

The Director was proud of his decisiveness, and when the weary committee approved the final wording, he indulged his self-congratulatory thoughts without any remorse about his involvement in the consultancy firm. After all, they had done a good job.

All of this was left unspoken in this current conversation with the Minister, except the urgent reiteration of the view that the Act prevented unethical research. That much of this was only possible on paper, and not in actuality, simply escaped his awareness, as indeed it had escaped the notice of everyone else.

'But what about Shakespeare?' asked the Minister. 'He's been dead all these years, surely we must have an easier way to make this kind of research possible without all the red-tape?'

'But that's the point, Minister,' said the Director, 'now we can know in advance whether a dead person is being maligned or not. And from what I know about Mr Zulu's research – and I am reading it right here on the internet – he is saying that Shakespeare was a Muslim. And so was Shaka.'

'What, Shakespeare a Muslim, and Shaka too? No, no, there were no Muslims in Shakespeare's time, that's unethical,' said the Minister, shaking her head in disbelief. 'I must tell the Principal that I cannot support her on this issue. Friendship is constant in all things, except in the office.'

'And that's why our Act is right just as it is, and all the universities must comply. Just the other day one of my monitors read about research being done at one of our premier universities, which tries to show that a butterfly flapping its wings in China can cause a hurricane here. We cannot spend good money on such nonsense. We should go to the media with Mr Zulu's Shakespeare garbage and let the public decide. We should not budge an inch.'

The anonymous email to Lucky simply said: Have you seen this? And a hypertext link directed Lucky to an article about babies dying in one of the government's hospitals.

The contents of the internet web page were translated into an audio document, which played like a voice recording. Lucky heard that generous donations of baby milk formula, given by an overseas donor company, Butterfly Baby, for our country's poor, was not so generous after all. The milk was banned in many countries when it was discovered to cause serious illnesses – and death in some instances – in babies and toddlers. The company went into a large-scale image cleanup mode and publicly acknowledged the problem and recalled every single can of milk powder. As the synthesized voice continued, Lucky found to his horror that the company had then struck a deal with the Director of Health to take the contaminated product (claiming that new research had disapproved the allegation of contamination) at a fraction of the original cost for use in government hospitals. Once again the Director's family and friends, with an overwhelming civic conscience, eagerly helped to transport the hundreds of thousands of cans of milk powder to hospitals around the country. And curiously, they could also be found for sale in shops where the more economically destitute communities lived. Such was the compassion of the Director and his family and friends.

Butterfly Baby, the gifting company from the far-away country, had had a clearance sale, and as Lucky saw, it was an unethical clearance.

'Thy ambition, thou scarlet sin, robb'd this bewailing land.' Lucky mentally noted the quotation from *Henry VIII*, which popped into his mind.

❧

Lucky forwarded the email to the Principal. The next day he received a call from the Faculty Administrator informing him that his name was on the graduation programme.

'Congratulations, Lucky, well done,' she said, sounding as if she was against the idiocy of the matter all along.

❧

After the doctoral citation was read at the graduation ceremony by a more relaxed, smiling Dean, whose performance management agreement was now back on track, Lucky received a standing ovation from the packed auditorium. With a beautiful volunteer at his side (and she sensed that her elegant, low cut dress was not wasted on this handsome and insightful young man), he walked unerringly to be capped by the Principal.

'You're lucky,' whispered the Principal, after capping the kneeling Lucky, resplendent in his red academic gown, with the sound of thunderous applause and ululating mothers drowning this slight exchange and keeping it just between the two.

'Yes, I'm Lucky Zulu,' was the comeback reply. 'Our remedies oft in ourselves do lie.'

'Yes, all's well that ends well,' smiled the Principal.

Lucky had fallen asleep with his cell phone in his hand (which he often used to listen to his email messages), so when it rang, the movement from outstretched hand to ear was immediate. And during that swift passage his thumb had already pressed one of the keys to receive the call.

'Hello,' he answered.

'Hello Lucky,' came the reply, announcing herself as the Faculty Administrator. 'Your application for a post-doctoral fellowship has been successful, provided you can show evidence of having submitted an article from your thesis to a high quality, international, peer-reviewed journal, which must be published in this subsidy cycle. And also, the journal must be accredited with our Ministry of Education.'

Lucky was about to respond, pointing out the absurdity of the request; absurd because it implied that he had a decent level of control over his article's acceptance and the time it would take to get into print; absurd because the literary journal that would accept the premise of his thesis and the scholarship on which it was based would in all likelihood be on the margins of mainstream discourse, and hence, not accredited. Scholars like him were still unpaving the way, widening the cracks of illusory certainty, but there was still a long road to travel. He was reminded of the fact that fuzzy logic was initially scorned by the mathematics establishment, who found it preposterous that the Aristotelian logic of self-contained opposites should be challenged by the absurd notion that something could be both itself and its opposite at the same time (How now, how now, chop-logic! What is this?), until technology and commerce in the East found great use for it. Only then did the dinosaurs of academia respond with any real semblance of intellectual inquiry.

But Lucky did not respond, because he saw so clearly that it was all a tale told by an idiot, full of sound and fury, signifying nothing.

ill will

The Twofold Tamil Rule

Prologue

If it had been assumed that this extraordinary but little-known ability that I possess was mine alone, one would be very mistaken. I was simply continuing in the tradition of a faraway time and a faraway place, when the need for retribution was just as great as mine.

So, I cannot proceed without context, without specifying how the past has determined the present, and how the present is going to determine the future.

This, then, is my story, of an unlikely history of three generations of unseen superheroes. I now realise that we were three generations of subversives, although not quite cast in the mould of fantastical American comic books, or even regarded as such by the more public figures of rebellion.

We were the shadows; the silent bearers of a power whose full and real face is only revealed by the telling thereof. We were the executors of the Twofold Tamil Rule.

One

Very simply, the Twofold Tamil Rule means that you must hit your adversary on the head, and, for good measure, you must hit him again. This action will grant you success. As a strategy it had gained such notoriety in certain circles that it is said that Winston Churchill once alluded to it in his famous 'We shall fight on the beaches...' speech. Apparently, after he had ended his wartime broadcast he covered the microphone with his hands and said, 'And if that doesn't work, we'll hit them over the head with bottles.'

But all this doesn't mean much if you don't know the exact nature and origins of the Twofold Tamil Rule; how it has featured in three generations of my family's history, and how it turned us into the shadowy subversives that we were.

☙

The history of the Twofold Tamil Rule was passed down to us by our late father who, although he had ample reason in apartheid South Africa to use the Rule, couldn't. It was passed down to him in turn by his mother, for, as this story will reveal, there was a good reason why he did not inherit it directly from his father. The history is bizarre, but I will tell it to you just as it was told to me.

The story starts in a little independent principality close to the Tanjore (or Thanjavur) district of the British-ruled Madras Presidency in South India in the mid 1890s, where the British Raj maintained a cantonment to supervise the local ruler.

In fact, there's something in the story of how the area was unofficially annexed that speaks to me of the rebellious character of my grandfather.

Apparently, while it was common knowledge that the British had colonised the port of Madras and used it as the centre of their vast sub-continental administration, the political elite of the principality felt that they were protected by the holy basil (Tulsi) tree, which for a long time was considered powerful, even against death. No Hindu home was without it, a practice which continues to this day, for it is a plant with wonderful medicinal properties. Unfortunately, people also thought it was magical. And they based this belief on the fact that the previous rulers of Tanjore, the Marathas from the north-western portion of the Deccan plateau, had refused to enter the principality on seeing the leaves and branches protecting the roads to the kingdom. But that was more than 200 years before, when magical thinking was especially rife. So, this fact, they reckoned, was enough protection against the British, for surely, like the warrior Marathas, they would not dare to march and ride on roads lined with branches from the holy tree? So certain were the Maharaja's advisors of this that they even forbade any armed resistance. My grandfather, then a young boy vigorously opposed to all traditional thinking, thought they were foolish, but they persisted in what became their grandest folly. The British marched and rode on their horses, and the leaves of the Tulsi trees withered in the sun. Magical thinking had failed, and wounded the people far more than the occupation by the British. But this act of gross stupidity ignited a passion for justice in my grandfather, who saw that the only way for him to become an effective subversive was to join the British cantonment.

My grandfather came from the village of *Pillai Manam*, inhabited mainly by a caste of agriculturists who adopted the surname Pillai which, in medieval times, was a title of honour bestowed on important court officials and aristocratic castes. The name was later adopted by the upwardly mobile agriculturists to distinguish themselves from the general peasantry. Some of these Pillais had been shepherds, and it is said that the constant counting of sheep was the reason for their evolution into accountants. They were highly sought after for their arithmetical skills by the wealthy merchant castes and, later, the British bureaucracy. It's no surprise, then, that the Twofold Tamil Rule is so precise in its formulation. And the name of the village is particularly significant to this story, because *manam* in Tamil, while perhaps having other meanings, also means 'mind'. 'Pillai's mind' is really the crux of this story. And *pillai* is also the Tamil word for 'child'.

Any army cantonment needs a good variety of accountant which, in the days of the British Raj, always entailed a combination of store-keeping and pay-master duties for the Indian accounting clerks. So, my grandfather, simply known as Pillai to his British superiors, joined the cantonment at the age of twenty, a position he earned because of his missionary education and his social rank in the community. He supervised the stores, kept a record of the stock and paid wages to the Indian labourers. The head accountant, the Englishman Shepstone, did very little, except preside over the monthly stipends paid to the British soldiers. It was thought improper for an Indian clerk like Pillai to deal directly with the white race in such intimate details like handing over money, so this was all that Shepstone ever did; he handed over money that was passed on to him by my grandfather.

My grandfather was particularly irritated by this sham exercise, because he reckoned that, except for skin colour, he and Shepstone were of equal rank. He deduced this, rightly or wrongly, from Shepstone's surname and profession which, in my grandfather's view, made them both shepherds in their distant past, and now accountants.

But my grandfather's almost ten-year presence in the army was a calculated strategy of a very subversive nature. Commanding great respect among the lower-ranking Indians in the cantonment, my grandfather enlisted the help of a few completely trustworthy men who helped him move stocks of grain and other produce into nearby villages to feed the destitute farmers and their families. These stocks would have been taken by the British as tax from the local farmers. The somewhat effete princely ruler had allowed this in return for so-called British protection. My grandfather allowed the men to keep a certain percentage for themselves as a way of acknowledging their continued support. What his long-term revolutionary plans were, nobody knows, and maybe simply feeding the poor, whose livelihoods were negatively affected by the presence of the British, was all that he intended to do.

Now here's the interesting part to this story. As storekeeper, my grandfather held the keys to the stores, so getting in at night was a relatively simple affair. All he and his aides had to do was bypass the sentry on duty, who was normally the alcoholic Barnes. On the nights of the monthly raid, my grandfather would ensure that Barnes received a bottle of wine, or some other alcoholic spirit, and by the time the raiding party arrived at midnight, he was usually in a drunken stupor.

However, there was an occasion when Barnes, inexplicably, had woken up and, hearing muffled sounds in the stores and seeing the door unlocked, went in to investigate. But he had barely entered the store when my quick-thinking grandfather, masked by the dark, picked up the nearest blunt object he could find and hit Barnes over the head. And to make doubly sure that Barnes was indeed unconscious, he hit him again. The object, it turns out, was a skittle, used in the much loved game by the officers in the cantonment, and also occasionally played by the prince and his courtiers.

There were two or three other occasions when Barnes was dealt this double blow, whereupon my grandfather became known affectionately as Two-Hit Pillai. Barnes invariably woke up the next morning with a sore head, but with no recollection of the night before, attributing his sorry plight to too much alcohol and vowing never again to drink Pillai's wine or spirits in one go. Unfortunately for my grandfather, Barnes eventually kept to his promise when temperance campaigners visiting the cantonment scared the wits out of him with their hellfire stories of alcohol and the devil. One particular remark that affected Barnes the most was about the sign of the devil that visited alcoholics – a cherry red nose. Barnes' bulbous nose was as cherry as you could get, and this fact left him less than cheery.

So, when Barnes heard sounds in the store on the fateful night that marks the start of my grandfather's lineage in South Africa, he was sober and suspicious. He walked in, rifle in hand, and demanded that the thieves show themselves. My grandfather reached for a skittle, but in the dark, he confused this with a rather firm aubergine (or *brinjal*), which was stacked next to the skittles with the other vegetables. Barnes not only brushed off the attack, but managed to raise the alarm with aubergine pulp dripping down his red nose. Most of the raiders were caught, but my grandfather, standing close to the door, slipped away.

Not knowing what the arrested men would reveal, my grandfather decided it was necessary to err on the side of caution and leave the area at once. There would be questions like the nature of the entry – there were no signs of a forced break-in – and he was a natural suspect as the only other holder of keys. They were also bound to check the stock records, and my grandfather's arithmetical genius would have come to light. He told fellow resistance workers and family that he was going to Pondicherry, the French enclave, and the hub of anti-British activism at the time. But, like his elder brother ten years earlier, he made his way to the port of Madras, where he boarded one of the ships taking paying passengers and cheap Indian labour to South Africa. He, of course, was a Pillai, and went as a paying passenger with enough money to hopefully join his brother in some kind of business venture outside a small coastal town in the Border district of the Cape Colony. Formerly known as British Kaffraria, my grandfather only later realised that he had jumped out of a British frying pan into a British fire. But it was on the passage to South Africa that the Twofold Tamil Rule took form.

ᘓ

South Indians were not the only passengers aboard the ship. There were also some North Indian merchants and other professionals like priests and vernacular language teachers, who were going to South Africa to start a new and hopefully more prosperous life. They had travelled all the way from various northern centres to catch this particular ship because it was carrying mainly 'passenger Indians', a term referring to those paying Indians travelling without passport to the Colonies of Natal and the Cape as citizens of the British Empire. Many came from the higher castes and would have heard of the disrespect for the caste system that prevailed aboard the ships, where Indians from vastly different linguistic and economic backgrounds encountered each other for the first time. With no segregation at mealtimes, some of the higher castes, passenger Indians as well as higher caste indentured labourers, balked at the idea of eating communally. They felt that it could result in the losing of their caste status, but I'm not sure whether they were referring to this life or the next.

Now my grandfather cut a dashing figure. Indeed, his tall physique and facial features, far removed from the stocky forms of most Tamils, suggest that he was indeed linked by ancestry, as he always claimed, to the warrior Nairs of Kerala, on the west coast of South India. And it was common for the aristocratic Nairs to be given the honorific title of Pillai for their services to state and king. The sequence of migratory events that merged my grandfather's lineage with that of the agricultural Pillais in Pillai Manam is completely unknown, however.

This aristocratic bearing was his passport to an inter-lingual and inter-racial relationship when he fell in love with the beautiful seventeen-year-old Meera, a Hindi-speaking landowner's daughter who was travelling with her paternal uncle to South Africa, ostensibly to get married into a family of wealth. Having lost her parents and youngest brother to a smallpox plague that ravaged her native district in the region of Bihar, Meera, the only daughter, was a burden to her two brothers, by virtue of the dowry system. They were struggling to survive on the meagre piece of land that they farmed, and which was now effectively owned by their uncle because of all the debt they had incurred. They were owners only in name.

My grandfather, fluent in Hindi as he was in many other Indian languages, found out that the paternal uncle wasn't really a blood relation, but put up a façade so as not to arouse suspicions among the higher ranking Hindus on board the ship. In fact, the 'uncle' was not only a prosperous landowner, but also a merchant who, after returning from a short visit to South Africa, decided that South Africa was a land of opportunity. He easily persuaded Meera's brothers to let her accompany him so that he could marry her into a wealthy family (he would take care of all her dowry expenses). This suggestion, given the complexities of the dowry system and its bearing on social status, was more than welcomed by the brothers. But his intentions were different. In his mid-fifties, this greasy, overweight and lecherous man was obsessed with the young maiden, and really wanted her as his concubine. And with his family thousands of miles away from him, his goal could be easily accomplished. In South Africa, he would have no one to answer to, and if questions were asked, he would simply say that she was his housekeeper or niece, whichever was appropriate at the time.

But Meera knew his intentions; he had as much as told her when he had had too much to drink and tried to paw and kiss her. All this she told my grandfather when they met secretly on one of the decks largely congregated by the labourers, where no questions would be asked. And he became enraged; another fact which supports his assertion that he was descended from the Pillai Nairs, a caste noted for their quick-temper and ferocity in war.

But the 'uncle', because of his vulgar display of wealth, attracted a small coterie of servants from the peasant castes, who accepted his financial favours in return for serving him. Some secretly hoped that they would continue this life of servitude with him when they settled in South Africa. One of their duties was to keep watch over Meera and to prevent any contact with my grandfather. On board the ship, the 'uncle' lorded over others in very much the way he ruled his little serfdom in Meera's district. In my grandfather's eyes, he was not an honourable man.

My grandfather felt imprisoned both by these tortuous circumstances and his inability to effect meaningful action. He was rendered impotent, and experienced again the rage that he had felt against the British until he joined the cantonment and carried out his audacious monthly raids.

Then the dreams began. First, he dreamt, night after night, about skittles. There was one night when his dream became a nightmare, when all the skittles transformed into grotesque-looking aubergines all looking like sentry Barnes' alcohol-enlarged nose – only the noses were a deep purple. Other than this single nightmare, these dreams made him feel empowered upon waking. He seemed to lose his sense of impotency, yet Meera was still hidden from him, and the delight of furtive conversations was now just a remembered whisper.

My grandfather was a man of figures and analysis. Although he was steeped in the spirituality of his culture, albeit in total abhorrence of the superstitious rituals of his religion, he was also a rational man, open to inquiry. So, he delved into the meaning of these dreams that gave him such strength. But his mind provided no answers, except that he was obsessed with skittles, until the day he passed by one of the seedy drunken servants on the deck who spat red-coloured spittle at him (the blood red colour was a consequence of chewing the much favoured betel nut, rather than the symptom of some dreaded disease). This was an outrage to my grandfather, not only because this uncultured, rude man was way below him in social rank, but also because he was one of Meera's captors. In an instant, without any volition on his part, my grandfather saw himself – in his mind's eye and in the most vivid way possible – hitting this beastly little man on the head with a skittle; not once, but twice. Almost as if watching a three-dimensional vision, the effect at the end was cathartic. My grandfather *knew* that something momentous had happened. But in that moment he didn't know what it was.

The next day, my grandfather found out. The spineless servant had come down with a mysterious ailment that made him a babbling wreck. And he felt that his condition was somehow linked to his ugly behaviour towards my grandfather, and incoherently called out his name, asking for forgiveness.

Meera's 'uncle' heard of the man's plight, also that he repeated my grandfather's name continuously. He became mildly worried about the assertions that my grandfather possessed psychic powers, which could bring a man down. But the 'uncle' was a man used to being in charge, so he decided to confront my grandfather, a man twenty-five years his junior, with taunts that he felt would wound him, taunts about Meera.

'You're just a bloody Madraji,' the 'uncle' said scornfully in Hindi, using the corruption of the name Madras as a signifier of race, 'and you want a fair Bihari girl for a wife. Who do you think you are?'

'I'm a Pillai,' my grandfather replied, somewhat imperiously.

And again my grandfather experienced the skittle sensation, which he later called the Twofold Tamil Rule, and again something happened. The 'uncle' was attacked by a virulent 'flu, and the severe bronchial spasms that accompanied the condition were helped neither by his weight nor by the other complications of obesity. In desperation, barely able to speak, he called for my grandfather,

'Pillai, Pillai,' he whispered wheezily, 'please take her. Take Meera, you can marry her. Just make me better. Please, brother, please.'

My grandfather, still uncomprehending of events, was nevertheless pleased with this new-found respect, and decided to use it to his advantage. He asked for the substantial dowry that the 'uncle' had promised he would pay Meera's groom. He then took half and told the 'uncle' to give the other half to Meera's brothers, in full.

'You cannot escape me,' my grandfather said with quiet assurance, as if he had been playing this particular role all his life. 'Ask anyone in my district about Two-hit Pillai. They'll tell you how I fooled the British for many years. Imagine what I can do to you. So you will go back to India as soon we land in South Africa, and give the money to Meera's brothers. You will also give them a letter that I will send with you. Tonight you will almost die. But tomorrow you will be better.'

My grandfather's last remarks were simply based on astute observation, that the 'flu had yet to run its course, and that the fever would get worse before it broke. Of course, he was guessing that the 'uncle' would survive; rather, he *thought* he was guessing. My grandfather, with Meera, money and jewellery, left the 'uncle'. As they left, my grandfather said in English, on impulse, 'Bye-bye.'

The 'uncle', hardly familiar with the nuances of the English language, especially spoken with an Indian accent, heard these words as *bhai, bhai* – 'brother, brother.' And in his state of acute fear, these words totally endeared my grandfather to the 'uncle' with visions of a full recovery.

And the next day the 'uncle' recovered, with great awe and respect for my grandfather.

It is said that when Meera's brothers received, two years later, a framed photograph of Meera and my grandfather, the 'uncle', hearing about it, called upon the brothers and paid them handsomely for a short- term loan of the picture. He then took this all the way to Calcutta, some three hundred miles away, to have copied, but in such a way that Meera's image was removed and only my grandfather's remained. This photograph was lavishly framed and decorated daily with fresh flowers. In that district of Bihar, Two-hit Pillai became quite famous.

CB

Two

Just before landing in the port of Durban, my grandfather, now married to Meera by way of a small ceremony conducted by one of the Brahmin priests on
board, briefly toyed with the idea of settling in this
fast-growing city, already home to many thousands
of his countrymen. Undeterred by the long arms of
the British Empire, he had heard about the political
work of the lawyer Mohandas Gandhi, and in fact
had read one of the issues of the *Indian Opinion*
which Gandhi had started publishing in 1904, two
years earlier, and which my grandfather had come
across in Pondicherry, en route to Madras. But this
idea was hastily abandoned when they disembarked.

As they stood in line waiting for customs clearance,
herded like sheep by the English port officials, my
grandfather noticed that the Tamil peasant in front of
him looked around furtively when asked his name by
the Tamil customs interpreter, and then said, 'Pillai'.

My grandfather almost choked in astonishment.
Here the evolution of the Pillai title was taking bizarre
forms, and in a silent rage he evoked the Twofold Tamil
Rule. The poor man in front fell forward with what
seemed to be acute abdominal pains. As he fell to
the ground he caught sight of my grandfather looking
wrathfully at him and realised that his deception had
been seen by the man whose fame as the possessor of
strange powers had spread like wildfire throughout
the ship.

'Not Pillai, not Pillai,' the writhing man screamed in Tamil, which my grandfather discerned from the dialect to be that spoken by village street sweepers. 'I'm Naidu, I'm Naidu.'

The peasant's new assertion of identity was equally false, but my grandfather let it pass, determined to leave Durban at once as his quick eyes scanned the list of passengers who had disembarked before him. There were so many Pillais and Naidus on the list (also spelt as Pillay and Naidoo by the English clerks), that my grandfather felt a mild nausea approaching.

'Bloody pariah Pillais,' said my grandfather to Meera, and in that moment he left a dubious legacy to his as yet unborn son, my father.

His apparent attitude of class towards what he called the pariah Pillais was perhaps not formed by the centuries-old Hindu conditioning of caste, which my grandfather with his sense of social justice found repugnant, but was perhaps more the conviction that you had to earn your place in society by the quality of conduct. He was not objecting to the Indian peasant calling himself Pillai on the grounds of caste or class or money; he was objecting on the grounds that a title that traditionally marked recognition for social services performed was being usurped. It was no different to a layman suddenly calling himself 'doctor'. Society, even now, does not tolerate such behaviour. And later we will come across other examples that show that perhaps this is how my grandfather really saw things.

Immediately my grandfather made arrangements to board a Union Castle ship for its two-day journey to a coastal town in British Kaffraria. And all the while, the beautiful Meera silently glowed in the shadow of her handsome saviour. She was simply content to go wherever he went.

€

When my grandfather and Meera arrived in the coastal town, they must have been overwhelmed by its signs of prosperous development. Tramcars already linked the Esplanade next to the harbour to the main street, and the town centre already sported fine buildings – like the imposing Victorian town hall – which looked to both my grandfather and Meera as grand as anything that they had seen in the British ports of Calcutta or Madras. For my grand-parents, their own rural localities, however rich in thousands of years of culture and tradition and sub-lime temple architecture, could not compare to the modernity that they encountered. That they should be so taken by this town's modernity is somewhat ironic, given that the town was a very late starter in industrial development. Although later awarded the dubious status of city, my father would always main-tain that it was a 'one-horse town'. He would also say, to give metaphoric variety, that it was like a bottle of soda water; too much fizz when you open it, then flat thereafter. But I'm putting the cart before the horse.

This coastal town was also the most racist in the Cape Colony, having persuaded the liberal Colonial Parliament in 1894 to adopt legislation against the Indians, such as forcing them into their own residential locations and disallowing them from walking on the sidewalks. In fact, this model of segregation was to become a blueprint in later years for the unified South Africa's racial segregation policy, called *apartheid*.

My grandfather's presence here seems, from the perspective of history, to be no coincidence, but more like an orchestration of events that had to do with the secret power he possessed to oppose anything that he considered unjust; in other words, I believe my grandfather was brought by destiny to this one-horse town to exercise the Twofold Tamil Rule and to lay the foundations for subversive activity against all forms of oppression. That this has indeed taken place through his issue will be picked up later in the story.

I alluded to destiny earlier, and certainly the synchronistic occurrences that my grandparents experienced must have made them believe in some kind of divine role in their lives. For Meera, my grandmother, this would have been framed by her simple religious faith; be pious to the gods and do your duty to your family and you will be blessed. For my grandfather, God was a vast inner reality, but only accessible through high moral conduct that one earned, like the lawyer Gandhi, through selfless social duty. This inner reality, when matched by outer deeds, produced these seemingly strange and beneficial occurrences.

And the divine hand (or the synchronistic event) was straightaway at hand when they disembarked. His elder brother, Ponnusamy, was there waiting for him, almost unbelieving when he saw my grandparents walking down the gangplank. And my grandfather was equally amazed – no, shocked – by the sight of his elder brother, who, he had come to understand, was a successful farmer living more than thirty miles from the town.

Tears rolled down my grandfather's cheeks as he embraced his elder brother, saying in Tamil, 'Brother, brother, we have come to be with you.'

Ponnusamy told my grandfather of the recurrent dream that forced him to come and meet this ship. He found it insane, he said, but he couldn't put it off as each dream left him restless with the knowledge that something important would occur at the harbour. The dreams were of the harbour, and ships, but there were no specific details about my grandfather.

And so Ponnusamy excitedly took my grandparents to a house that he rented in the town for their monthly visits to the market that actually lasted a week.

And there, at the house in The Lane, Clarke's End – which he and my grandfather would eventually buy along with a few others – my grandparents met Ponnusamy's coloured wife Lilly and their two children, whom I only knew as Uncle Harold and Aunty Edna. Apparently they had Tamil names as well, but Ponnusamy, as the only Indian in a mixed marriage in the farming district, did not insist. He had the foresight to blend in.

Apparently this inter-racial union, a heresy in India, was immediately accepted as utterly normal by my grandparents. But then, my grandfather had a Hindi-speaking wife, which was equally heretical.

'I don't know why, but I like her when I first meet her. She was like mother to me. Later I hear others call Lilly bushman, but she speak Tamil better than me. What bushman?' my grandmother would tell her children whenever she recounted their extraordinary arrival in the town.

And yes, Lilly spoke Tamil with a slightly quaint accent, obviously well tutored by Ponnusamy, just as my grandfather had made Meera fully tri-lingual. But to her children she spoke an unknown language that my grandfather later discovered was Dutch. Ponnusamy spoke Tamil and some English to his children.

ᘓ

My grandparents' arrival was a blessing to Ponnusamy and his family. They were exhausted by the monthly travels from the farm to the town, and with the increasing hostility towards the few Indian farmers by the white farmers, especially at the town market, Ponnusamy had the idea to supply the many Indian fruit and vegetable hawkers through a kind of Indian farmers' collective. The failure of this idea is central to the story of the Twofold Tamil Rule.

Ponnusamy set my grandfather up as his agent

and liaison man with the local hawkers, and my grandparents were ready to start a new life. In many ways, with the large storeroom at the back of the house packed with fruit and vegetables, my grandfather felt right at home. Only the skittles were missing.

℘

Within two years they had a child, a girl, Ambika, but my father was only born eight years later in 1916.

Life moved along smoothly for the threesome and the extended family that came along once a month, but the need for the Twofold Tamil Rule outside the home became increasingly necessary.

My grandmother, and later my aunt, told numerous stories of how little favours were enacted for the poorer Indians who were prejudiced in so many ways by the many racist whites who wanted the 500 or so Indians out of the town. There was the German stall owner's wife, Heidi, who shouted 'filthy coolie, filthy coolie' at Vellu, the kindly peanut vendor, every time he visited the market for supplies. She detested Vellu, it was said, because his roasted peanuts were far superior to hers, having used secret spices to flavour his much sought after 'monkey nuts' as they were fondly called. Also, his cheaper price put her out of contention in the peanut selling business at the beachfront on weekends. She envied Vellu's success, even though she and her husband Franz had a permanent stall at the market, while Vellu barely scraped a living from his peanut selling at the beach and at the local park. She got her comeuppance when she and her family were forced out of town by the English during the anti-German sentiment that accompanied the First World War.

Then there was Simjee, the small rag-and-bone man, who had the idea to start a garage selling petrol in the growing boom of motor vehicles that was taking place. He was led to believe by the Port Master Kirby that he was buying barrels of oil from a wrecked ship, but found out that he had bought many thousands of nails en route for the colonies. My grandfather persuaded him to keep the nails and he didn't have to wait too long for the Rule to strike. When the war broke out in 1914, there was such a shortage of nails in the country that Simjee became, by today's standards, a millionaire, buying up as much property as could in Clarke's End. He and his large family lived in the grandest house in the area, until Clarke's End was eventually destroyed by apartheid. And when Kirby lost his job and almost became destitute because of other charges of fraudulent activities as Port Master, he rented one of Simjee's houses in Clarke's End. As a white of his social standing, it was a big drop in status to live in this mixed area. When he asked Simjee for the house, Simjee realised that he had nailed him, but also recognised the part that he had played, albeit unwittingly, in his good fortune, and never charged him rent. Simjee also particularly relished the fact that a white man like Kirby was obligated to him.

Years later, Simjee, a devout Muslim, was to give his blessing when one of his daughters married my father's cousin, Harold, a Hindu who embraced the Christian faith in fairly equal measure, a trait in Clarke's End that was to characterise many offspring of mixed marriages. Simjee never forgot the good fortune that came with the Twofold Tamil Rule.

When my grandfather had the idea to create a place of worship for the Tamil-speaking Hindus, the proposal was vehemently opposed by Crompton, one of the more conservative municipal councillors, who railed at my grandfather with accusations of blasphemy and witchcraft. On the day of the final municipal deliberations, it was well known that his vote would be the deciding one, with many liberal councillors voting for or abstaining, either having the good sense to see through such nonsense, or afraid that Gandhi's civil disobedience campaigns in Durban would reach these shores. On that very day Crompton had a mild heart attack and the temple consecrated to Lord Shiva came into being. The timing of events did not go unnoticed by the city fathers, and when the Gujerati-speaking Hindus and the Muslim community applied for their own places of worship, permission was granted with no fuss. It is believed that, for reasons of health, Crompton returned shortly afterwards to his birthplace in Neasden outside London, now home to the largest traditional Hindu temple outside India. Prince Charles has proclaimed it a national monument, furthermore. But if unlikely Neasden boasts this imported religious symbol, Clarke's End no longer does so: the forces of apartheid burned down the Tamil temple some six decades later in order to force the Indians to relocate to an Indians-only location and also to make way for a highway. By law, places of worship could not be touched by the segregationist policies of apartheid, so the enactors of one of the most pernicious social systems in the world found other means.

The Twofold Tamil Rule was not confined to fearful whites, however. Once, my grandfather came upon a group of five Indian youths all sporting the boat-shaped Gandhi cap. It was 1914, and Indian morale in the Union of South Africa was high after Gandhi had won considerable concessions for them through his passive resistance campaigns. These youths, presumably on their way from a vernacular language class, were taunting a ragged-looking African boy and throwing the odd stone at him.

'Kaffir, bloody dirty kaffir,' the adolescent boys shouted, their accents still heavily tied to their origins in India, although all of them would have been born in their adopted country.

'Stop, boys, stop, this is not right,' said my grandfather, knowing many of them and their families by sight. But like the madness that infects crowds who suddenly attain power, however briefly, the boys turned on my grandfather.

'Shut up, Madraji, you're dirty just like this kaffir,' they said, seemingly totally oblivious of his standing in the Indian community and, moreover, totally oblivious of the irony of their dress and what it represented. 'You and your pretty Bihari wife, soon the Market Master will take her.'

The young men's behaviour incensed my grandfather, and the reference to the Market Master was the last straw.

'You're all shit,' said my grandfather, 'you're all shit', and he walked away. The boys would have been totally mistaken if they understood the remark as a depiction of their character. The repeated formulaic phrasing was actually very literal.

The young men were still jeering at both my grandfather and the African boy, when one of them, the hawker Jeevanbhai's son, complained of a sudden stomach pain. He indicated that he needed the toilet urgently, but before he could take any action, his white pyjama pants were stained by his uncontrollable bowel movements. The other boys quickly followed a similar fate and the stench and staining that marked them brought howls of laughter to their victim, the young African boy, who quickly drew the attention of passers-by to what must have been one of Clarke's End's most bizarre incidents.

Most of the boys were never seen in public again, and all received canings from their fathers for their treatment of my grandfather. Whether they were really in sympathy with the African boy is doubtful. And how the boys came to the pejorative term 'Madraji' was a matter that was never raised, and I suspect that my grandfather felt that what went on behind closed doors should be kept there for the sake of communal peace. I was to have this very same label thrown at me at school more than five decades later, however, showing that the racial attitudes of the motherland continued in whispers in some homes. Then it was a schoolboys' argument.

'I'm a Hindu,' said my friend Bharat to me, both of us in standard four and about eleven years old.

'I'm also a Hindu,' I replied.

'No you're not,' came the indignant reply. 'You're a Madraji.'

That was the first time that I had heard the word. I was incensed because of the imprecision of the terms.

'Listen, I am a Tamil and I'm also a Hindu. You're a Gujerati and also a Hindu.' But this made no sense to Bharat.

Later I was to find that the Hindu Tamils enacted their own absurdity. They referred to Hindu Tamils as Tamils, but could not see that the Tamils belonging to the Christian religion were also Tamils, just practising a different faith. One of the ironies of this was that many of the Christian Tamils could still speak the language, with one of the sects continuing to worship in Tamil, while Tamil as a spoken language was barely evident among the Hindus. The Hindu worshippers of my generation could sing the great Tamil hymns totally unaware of the meaning of the words. But let's get back to the Market Master.

Market Master Henry Jones was another matter.

47

A former seaman with the British Navy, he was yet another import into this African landscape, uniquely marked by the fact that all its rulers, including the present ones, are descended from peoples fleeing some sort of oppression in their native lands. The original inhabitants, one of the First Peoples, the Khoi-San, were systematically decimated by successive waves of colonisers. The truth is, we are all colonisers. And Henry Jones was a particularly colourful one.

Coming as he did from a line of fruit and vegetable merchants associated with London's famed Covent Garden, Jones, in this small town of few skilled people, took on the job he was most familiar with – managing the market. This may not have been a natural role for someone of his social rank in his native London, however. More likely he would simply have been a vendor. But we cannot deny him this rise in function. The Indians would also benefit immensely, freed from the shackles of a society that was doubly stratified by Hindu caste and British colonialism.

As Market Master, Jones held considerable power in the allocation of stalls, openly favouring the English-speaking farmers over the Germans and totally sidelining the few Indian farmers, like Ponnusamy, who had to sell their produce outside the market square. This actually backfired on the white farmers because it meant that the customers of the market – the townspeople and the hawkers – were first met by the Indians, at least on the side where the Indians set up stalls. It was one of those situations where segregation actually benefited the Indian farmers because of this unhindered contact. And this scenario gave rise to Ponnusamy's plan for a completely separate Indian market, which he suggested should be close to the former location designated for Indians, quite far from the town centre and white business.

Ponnusamy saw that such a location for an Indian market would be very advantageous. There would be no competition from the white farmers, and naturally the hawkers, mainly Indian, would support their fellow Indians. Furthermore, the former Indian location was now inhabited by very poor whites, Afrikaner refugees from the Anglo-Boer war, who were probably even more despised by the English than the Indians were. This community would also be ready supporters.

The idea put the mainly racist municipal councillors into an awful quandary, with Ponnusamy playing to their segregationist aspirations. He openly stated, as a matter of strategy, that they were prepared to move back to the Indian location, knowing full well it was virtually impossible to effect. The whites had long wanted the Indians to live in Willet's Estate, as it was called, far on the western end of the town. And they almost achieved their plan, with almost all of the 500 or so Indians living there by 1904 because of the legislation that was passed in 1895, until the Indians found a loophole that brought them all back into the town, mainly into Clarke's End. If they could afford to rent a house with no more than six tenants for the princely sum of seventy-five pounds per annum, a huge amount of money in those days, then they could stay in the town. And most of the Indians did. In fact, greed has a way of knocking down laws, and many whites in Clarke's End, discovering that they were not accountable to the municipal by-law which restricted plot sizes to one acre, eagerly sub-divided their plots into ten sub-divisions and built little homes to rent to the Indians. Simjee and others like Ponnusamy and my grandfather were to buy these homes when legal ownership of land was allowed to Indians, at a later time when it was reluctantly accepted that Clarke's End was now the unofficial Indian location, but also occupied by coloureds and a few blacks, many of them tenants of Indian owners.

Ponnusamy's suggestion, it seems, came at the right time. The municipality couldn't move the poor whites, and yet the Indians seemed to be arguing for segregation that was law. This infuriated both Jones and Williamson, who was the very racist newly-elected ward councillor for Clarke's End, and a former British Indian army officer.

That's when the British genius for 'divide and rule' suddenly entered the fray with Williamson and Jones' enacting their ancient roles of master and servant. The unscrupulous, pompous Williamson was aware of the married Jones' sexual adventures with some of the female stallholders and hawkers across the colour line, often using his position of authority to effect all kinds of beneficial deals for the women, some of them married, in exchange for sexual favours. He suggested to Jones that if he didn't want a fate similar to Kirby's, the disgraced Port Master who now lived, in Williamson's words, 'like a dog in one of Simjee's ramshackle coolie houses', then he needed to stop Ponnusamy and his brother. Williamson implied that Jones had to disgrace the Pillai brothers by sleeping with their wives, knowing full well, from his experience in India, what this would do to the brothers and their standing in the community.

But Ponnusamy's wife was a homemaker living mainly on the farm and therefore not in any kind of contact with Jones, while unfortunately Meera, as my grandfather's business aide, was. And Jones lusted after the beautiful Meera, who was unapproachable. Jones had had a liaison with two or three Indian women, and not everything had to do with Jones' economic hold over them. Jones, when he wanted, could be very charming and had roguish good looks and race on his side to lure the women; some of whom were trapped in loveless, arranged marriages, and exposed to abusive husbands, many of whom were alcoholics. The many fair Indians in Clarke's End have their roots in this very market.

'It's not going to work, guv,' said Jones to Williamson, 'Pillai's wife, she's just too high and mighty, bloody wog.'

'Iago, stupid man, Iago,' replied Williamson cryptically.

'Iago?' asked the puzzled Jones.

'Yes, you know, Shakespeare,' said Williamson. 'You don't have to do the deed, just suggest that something could have happened. That should get to Pillai. Iago used a handkerchief.'

Jones, after being told the part that the handkerchief played in Othello's downfall, took Williamson literally and planted one of his own monographed handkerchiefs in Meera's bag. When Meera found it, she showed it to my grandfather, who immediately suspected some kind of malicious conniving. He evoked the Twofold Tamil Rule.

The next day Jones developed a rather nasty-looking running ulcer on his groin, but unaware of Two-hit Pillai and his reputation, he interpreted the sudden eruption as the wrath of God coming down on him for his sexual misadventures. He hurriedly told Williamson that he was backing out of the plan, and that the bloody Indians could have their market.

And it would have been the case, had luck not favoured the loathsome Williamson. He chanced upon a copy of the Crown Minutes for the Port of Natal, wherein it was mentioned that the British Government of India was looking for a number of nationalist agitators believed to be hiding in the Colony of Natal in the wake of Gandhi's political gains. It was 1918, the Great War was over, and the British were now focused on putting out minor fires that had started in their colonies. Effectively they had lost South Africa in 1910, and they were damned if they were going to lose India, the jewel in the crown.

In those minutes my grandfather was listed, complete with a physical description.

In his stately office, modelled after a colonial men's club, where he presided over his growing business empire, which stretched far into the hinterland, Williamson confronted my grandfather.

'You're finished, Pillai, you're finished. I want you and your family out of here, or I'll hand you over to the police for deportation. You understand? Bloody coolie troublemaker. You've got a month.'

Williamson was clever enough to realise that handing my grandfather over to the police would not necessarily put an end to the Indian market issue. There was still the brother Ponnusamy and the others. But this offer allowed my grandfather to keep his family and stay in South Africa, if he so wanted, provided he and his brother left town for good.

'I understand,' said my grandfather. And then, as is the case with a trapped animal, an intense rage overcame him, a rage that almost bypassed every moral sense that had made him such a good man. 'You... suffer, you English bastard, you suffer.'

My grandfather almost said 'die', but that curse violated his deepest sense of human connection and, also, he didn't know if the Twofold Tamil Rule allowed such an unholy act.

Williamson only laughed at him; there was no context for fear. 'You stupid, superstitious coolie, do you honestly think I can be harmed by your silly threats? Get out of here, and out of my town. Now!'

My grandfather only told Meera about the encounter. To tell Ponnusamy would compromise the market action, and he would only do so if and when it was certain that no other options existed. There was also the fear that Williamson may have told others in the council about my grandfather's true identity. My grandfather was a worried man.

When, through discreet enquiries, he found that Williamson was hale and hearty, my grandfather fell into a deep, brooding depression, which alternated with obsessive, vengeful thoughts about Williamson over which he had no control.

'God will help us, don't worry,' said my grandmother placatingly, relieved that it was still a week until Ponnusamy and his family returned to the town with their load of produce for the monthly market sales. But my grandfather did not reply.

The great 'flu of the time was still sweeping the country, and the worry, fear and intense feelings of hate that he felt continually now for Williamson made my grandfather very susceptible to the ravages of this 'flu. And he succumbed.

My grandmother now prayed that Ponnusamy would arrive early. My grandfather's condition worsened with doctors seemingly impotent against the onslaught. For the protection of the family, they insisted that he be kept isolated, an order that my grandmother found difficult to heed, relying on her faith instead to keep her from harm. But the children were not allowed near him. He was constantly feverish, frequently calling out in Tamil for his mother, but most of the time cursing Williamson.

Then, my grandmother heard that Ponnusamy and his family were due anytime. Their wagons had been spotted a day's journey from the town by Simjee, the only Indian to own a motor car. She felt a burden drop from her shoulders.

And that night the fever broke. When she went into the dark room to give him some hot soup, he sounded at ease. He held her hand tenderly before letting her go back to the children.

At about ten o' clock that evening, for the first time in days, they heard him get up to go to the bathroom. Then what happened afterwards is a blur. My grandmother heard a terrifying scream, and what seemed to be the words, 'Meera, Meera... what... come.' Then they heard a loud fall onto the wooden floor.

My grandmother rushed to the bathroom, to find my grandfather lying dead, a look of utter terror on his face; a look that only receded with the mysterious movement of death itself.

გვ

My grandmother would later say that he called out, saying that death had come. But in the interpretations of my paternal aunt Ambika, the story of her father's death changed to suit the occasion of telling. Sometimes he simply died from the effects of 'flu, sometimes he saw death approaching, but most times he was visited by a ghost. She deduced the latter from the word 'come'.

'He was saying,' she would say, authoritatively, brooking no counter argument, 'Meera, see what ghost has come'. These ghosts would be my Edwardian aunt's great weapon of fear over her family for many decades, as she, like my father, fought to exorcise the demons left by their father's mysterious death. So the ghost version became the official explanation, which grew slowly and incrementally into a family legend that bore little resemblance to what I first heard as a child. The ghost of my grandfather's death was now that of a deranged Muslim fakir who drained the blood from living black fowls with no discernable wounds. But it was a perversion of the truth that simply drained many of us of our commonsense.

೮੪

My grandmother, as was the custom then, was adopted by Ponnusamy as his second wife, and they had one child together. Lilly was totally accepting of this situation and, by and large, they lived as a close-knit family. The Indian market was eventually obtained with full municipal permission, because Williamson, unexpectedly, also succumbed to the 'flu and died on the day of my grandfather's memorial service, sixteen days after his death. On this sixteenth day, it is said that the soul returns to its source. My grandmother would say that my grandfather had taken Williamson with him. Ponnusamy eventually leased the farm and started a successful general dealer's business in the town.

My grandmother told only my aunt and father about the Twofold Tamil Rule. Not even Ponnusamy was told its history as I have done here. And they told their children. And only my brother and I took it seriously.

Three

'Tell him I'll give two kicks up his backside,' my father would invariably shout to Charlie, the Xhosa boy who grew into a man as a member of our household. And Charlie, huge and round, would just have a hearty laugh. He had heard the threat so many times, that even he would later adopt it as a favoured expression, of course without any historical context. When my father died, it would also be Charlie's way of carrying my father's flag, of expressing a simple, deep affection that could not be articulated.

But that's what the Twofold Tamil Rule had transformed into: ineffectual threats, because my father had been bound.

It transpired that neither of my father's siblings had inherited the ability that my grandfather had wielded so effectively. My aunt, particularly, despite her love of ghosts and the supernatural, was bypassed by the mysteries of natural selection, but the Twofold Tamil Rule manifested with great vigour in my father, at a time when he had neither the maturity nor the social context for its use. So he had to be bound.

As a young man in a town suddenly finding some semblance of economic direction – with the Great War two decades earlier softening racial edges as South Africans of colour joined their white fellowmen against the German forces – it would have been easy to believe, in this big town with pretensions of being a city, that the country was moving towards racial equality. But my father and others like him were caught in an illusion, an illusion peculiar to the town. Its size meant the races were in close proximity to each other, and in Clarke's End in particular, the Indians, coloureds and whites had settled into an easy existence with many mixed marriages being the norm. And the Indian merchants were prospering. For my father, it was time to make his mark.

My father's name was Raju, but known to everyone as Raj, an appropriate name given his princely good looks inherited from both his parents. With his knack of making money and his charming personality, he led a life, literally, of wine, women and song. But wine did not mix with the Twofold Tamil Rule.

One night, when he was quite 'on', his sister spotted him trying to sneak into his bedroom. She called their mother and this infuriated my father. Before long, cups and saucers and anything moveable crashed inexplicably to the floor waking up the extended family. My aunt was quick to label it an invasion by malevolent spirits, but my grandmother saw that it was a new expression of the Rule, now under the influence of a tantrum and alcohol. So, a prominent fakir from Cape Town was summoned, no doubt the son of the same fakir whose ghost years earlier would drain the blood of live fowls. Now the son was going to drain some of my father's life.

The wiry fakir, it is said, enacted an elaborate ritual, which required my father being kept in his room for three days and three nights, with just the fakir permitted to see him with his assortment of talismans and his trademark black fowl kept in a hessian bag. Their large house resonated with strange, other-worldly sounds as the fakir intoned religious scriptures to bind the Rule forever. And after the three days had passed, my father emerged, subdued. It's not known whether it was the actual efficacy of the rituals or the belief in them that bound the Rule, but a raging tiger was trapped to later became a parody of itself; it was now 'two kicks up the backside', but really words without effect. And my father never ever spoke about his experiences of confinement in the room.

But not all of the Rule was bound, however. My father was extremely intuitive and this ability played out well for him as one of the biggest and most modern businessmen in Clarke's End, competing directly with similar white businesses in Main Street. His business was a combination of jeweller and hardware store, and while this unusual mix may seem strange to those accustomed to the white tradition of specialist stores, it was still tied to the character of the small Indian shops known as general dealers, where they literally sold a little of everything, including illegal alcohol. But with my father, the Indian shop had evolved. It had become a modern business in layout and in practice. And the other Indian shopkeepers respected him for this. They were unable to break free because most had no skills to make more of their corner shops, while my father had learnt the trade of watch repairing, which allowed him to evolve. And he was proud of this. Until Tommy Narayadu appeared in town.

Tommy Narayadu looked like an Indian mix of Charlie Chaplin and Hitler, with a sneering quality that accompanied his distinctive, affected 'white' accent. And, from my father's point of view, he dared to do the unthinkable. He opened a business equally as modern as my father's, but specialising in sophisticated electronic gadgetry that had no customers in Clarke's End – although it was a fascinating place for the boys of the area with the advent of the James Bond films. Tommy Narayadu had his regular clientele among the whites, especially as he offered an item that was fast becoming a necessity in the more affluent areas – burglar alarms.

Tommy Narayadu made my father's blood boil, an expression that I've always associated with my father, and rooted in a more literal fact – he had high blood pressure. My mother would tell my father to stop being so envious, a remark that would really send my father's blood boiling, but my father always felt that there was something more than that. True, Tommy remarked to my father, when he first paid a courtesy visit to all the local businessmen, that he was actually a Pillai from Durban, but preferred to use his father's name, as was the proper South Indian way (a statement made with that sneering 'know it all' attitude of his).

'Bloody pariah Pillai,' my father said when Tommy Narayadu had left, his father's ancient disdain surfacing in these modern times.

'Oh, leave the man alone,' my mother would frequently implore, quite taken with Tommy Narayadu's sophistication and knowledge, which was very evident in the kind of business he was running. And my father's blood would boil.

My father's resentment was not without some basis in fact. After a couple of years of trading quietly in the area, Tommy Narayadu suddenly became involved in the Chaker's End Association, a rather powerless body that presented basic civic concerns to the city council, and which became somewhat

61

more active when the more affluent coloureds were given their own residential area which removed many of them from the congested out rooms of small Clarke's End houses. Then the Association was used as an intermediary by the council to settle squabbles over the awarding of plots and the many claims that municipal officials were being bribed to favour one applicant over the other.

When Tommy Narayadu came into the Association, it was now largely an Indian body, most of the serving coloured officials having left for their new homes in their new area. Tommy Narayadu then suggested that the Indians start agitating for their own area, away from the squalor of Clarke's End.

No one disputed that parts of Clarke's End had degenerated into a slum, but it was always assumed that the Indians, under the sweeping movement of apartheid, would simply be allowed to upgrade their homes now that the coloureds had left. And anyway, there was no vacant area available in the city.

'That's not true,' said Tommy Narayadu, always in control no matter how rowdy the public meetings sometimes became. 'The Africans are being moved to the new location outside the city, and their village, I am told, will be made available to us. Come people, how many of us want to continue living with our parents and grandparents in two and three bedroom houses, many falling apart, while we have growing families of our own? Let's be sensible about this. We can't stop apartheid, and anyway, we Indians have always liked living on our own. And if we don't act soon, we could lose out. Look where they put the coloureds, in the goddamn hills, but the old African village is still part of town'.

For the second time in his life, Ganny 'Dagga' Dadoo stood up in this packed cinema auditorium, his middle nickname being a reference to his fondness for a certain *Cannabis sattiva*; also known as marijuana, pot or grass. The first time was a few years earlier when, during the screening of *The Dirty Dozen*, a message was flashed onto the screen: 'Ganny "Dagga" Dadoo, the police are waiting for you outside'. On that occasion, the crowd were playfully boisterous in getting Ganny to leave because they were annoyed by the flashing message which interfered with their enjoyment of twelve misfits taking on the might of the Nazis. But they also supported Ganny's open defiance of the law which forbade the weed of his choice; dagga smoking became a kind of underground symbol of subversion against the police state. Now, in this community meeting, the outcast Ganny was doing a reprisal of his role, mixed with the heroics of *The Dirty Dozen*.

'I'm not moving to no bloody village' said the usually reticent Ganny. 'Have you seen the place? It's a sewer.'

Ganny had touched on a common perception; that the village was a maze of dirt streets indistinguishable from the open sewerage system where the stench of human excrement characterised the location of the city's most disadvantaged citizens. In Ganny's mind, as indeed it would have been in the minds of others, this was where the Indians were being moved. It was intolerable.

'I've got my roots here,' said an earnest Ganny. This statement drew wild laughter from the crowd, because most associated 'roots' with Ganny's known patch of dagga plants somewhere in the overgrown backyard of Aunty Poonima's house, which doubled up as the local shebeen, Clarke's End's premier haven of illegal liquor. It was said that Aunty Poonima had bought off certain corrupt members of the police force who provided protection against any police raids, while other shebeen owners were not so lucky. But Aunty Poonima was lucky for Ganny and he reciprocally returned the favour by providing her clients with a bigger range of stimulants. All this would be gone if Clarke's End was destroyed.

'Have you seen the size of the homes being planned for those of us who can't afford to build?' boomed the voice of burly Subri Thomas, the city's first unofficial Indian motor mechanic, at a time when the country's people of colour were paralysed by the horrendous job reservation law which reserved certain trades – electricians, plumbers, motor mechanics, etc. – for whites only. But Subri had defied the law and operated brazenly from his back yard. That he had maimed a few trade inspectors who tried to shut him down brought him great respect.

'I won't be able to get my king size bed into the

main bedroom,' said Subri. 'What do they expect me to do, break down the wall? I'll break their fuck-ing heads!'

Subri's expletive, common to his speech, empow-ered the crowd, and they cheered him on.

'Let them try to move me. I'll hit them with my bare hands, and if that doesn't work, I'll hit them on their heads with the biggest spanner that I've got. And look at the quality of their houses. In the coloured area I saw a house where the electrical pipe was six inches away from the wall. When I asked the electrician why the pipe was so far from the wall, he said they moved the wall. Anyone with bright eyes can see that they're using low grade contractors.'

Subri's remarks had turned the meeting into an impromptu comic routine, where humour, as in the great protest theatre that was spurned by the country's anti-apartheid activism, played its subversive role of satirising and alleviating pain.

But Tommy Narayadu was smooth, and he coun-tered the criticisms rationally and made points that were appealing. The newer generation of Indians, many of them professionals like teachers and doctors and accountants, were living in cramped houses, some secretly hoping for a death to make a house vacant. This hope was not entirely without logic. One death in Clarke's End was invariably followed by two or three others within a very short space of time. It's inexplicable, but the records can prove this. Moreover, these deaths followed a distinct pattern; the death of a Hindu Tamil was followed by the deaths of other Hindu Tamils. Similarly, Christian Tamils died in clusters, as did Hindu Gujeratis. But this was not an effective way to solve a housing shortage. And Tommy Narayadu knew this.

'OK, Tommy,' my father said at the public meeting held in the local cinema then known as a bioscope, 'I can see that we need more space, but why should those of us who already own homes in Clarke's End move? We've been here since about 1904. Our schools, temples and churches are here.'

'Good point,' said Tommy, always agreeing with everyone in a way that masked his deeper motives. 'But let's in principle accept the new area, without committing ourselves to giving up Clarke's End. And let's get the best deal that we can.'

That last remark drew appreciative applause from the crowd, and so, in principle it was agreed to inform the city council and the Department of Community Affairs – the actual executor of the government's apartheid policies – that the Indian community would accept the African village as their new location, with very few realising the historical irony; that the new location was just above the original location planned for the Indians at the beginning of the century, now called Willet's Estate and occupied by the poor whites often referred to as 'railway whites'; a label that would identify the Afrikaner government's policy of uplifting the poor rural Afrikaners by giving them jobs in the railways.

CR

My father was uneasy after the last public meeting of the Association. He became brooding, prone to temper tantrums with frequent 'I'll kick him up the backsides'. He sensed that something was amiss. So, he phoned his old friend from the police who was now working as a private investigator – Jacob Hart.

'Jacob, what the hell is going on with Clarke's End and the group areas?' my father asked the man he had befriended almost a decade earlier, when at that time Jacob was investigating Clarke's End's only armed robbery.

'I'll find out, Raj, and get back to you,' said Jacob.

And when Jacob came back with the results of the investigation, my father's blood boiled.

'You're not going to be allowed to keep Clarke's End,' he said. 'And Tommy Narayadu knows this. He's working for them, Raj. Trained by the security branch in electronics and sent here to destroy the last mixed area in South Africa. If you've had anything installed by him, be careful, they could be listening. And your temple is in the middle of the planned new highway. But I don't know how they're going to get around that one.'

My father, as chairman of the Temple, immediately called a meeting, but invited the rest of the community as well. To call an Association meeting meant going via Tommy Narayadu, who was secretary, and

67

my father did not want to alert him to what he was going to expose.

The Temple meeting was well attended. My father was blunt.

'Ladies and gentlemen, that bastard Tommy Narayadu is working for the security branch and Community Development,' my father burst out, oblivious of the fact that he was speaking in a place of worship. Without naming his source, but displaying crucial council minutes, which Jacob had obtained, my father showed the people of Clarke's End how they had been duped.

The football crowd in the meeting was furious, and agitated that Tommy Narayadu be given the hiding of his life, notwithstanding the fact that one of the prestigious football trophies was the Tommy Narayadu Floating Trophy, in the shape of a ball emerging from an electronics circuit board.

But everyone was too late. Tommy Narayadu's shop and the house behind it were empty, as if he and his small family had never existed. And when the local newspaper carried the story, there were no comments from either the security branch of the police force, or the Department of Community Development. Within a month houses in Clarke's End were evaluated for purchase by Community Development, and the owners were notified of impending payouts, based not on the actual value of the buildings, but solely on the municipal valuations of the land; valuations which were way, way below the market value. Clarke's End, as everyone was to later discover, was to become a light industrial area with many plots already taken up, in my father's words, 'for next to nothing', by white businessmen, many of whom were in the city council.

〇3

My father made a few feeble legal gestures to get the Department of Community Development to pay him more for his house based on the extensive renovations that he had made over the years, but to no avail. They would not budge. He was crushed, dragged down more by the knowledge that his spirit, deep down, had been bound all those many years ago, during a time of youthful licentiousness, and was now totally without power.

It was the Christmas holidays when he sent my mother and younger brother for a vacation to Durban. I was to accompany him later when the business closed for a week in the New Year.

But on the eve of the New Year something in him altered. He had received payment for the property in the post. He paced the house, the place of his birth, for hours, going from room to room, speaking to unseen people, the spirits of his past. I heard him speak Tamil for the first time in my life, imploring his mother to do something. But I did not understand everything. Then he made me play his favourite music; Tamil devotional songs to Lord Shiva and his son Muruga; songs that still resonate with me. Then, just before midnight, he lay down on his bed and called for Charlie and me. With tears streaming down his eyes, he whispered:

'Give them the Twofold Tamil Rule. Don't do what I did. Ask your Aunty Ambika, she'll tell you everything. And tell your brother.'

He turned to Charlie and said, 'Look after the boys. You're like my own son.'

And then he paused, before saying his last words to me, 'I love you all, my boy…love…'

In the lounge the cabinet record player, finished in mock imbuia and later to be overshadowed by my father's casket, was still playing the devotional songs. As if to mark the passage of time, an ancient, resonant chant that spoke of the timeless filled our home.

Four

It would be another six years before I met my aunt Ambika, now living in London with her daughter and grandchildren – part of the new wave of Indian emigration following a causal pattern of the colonised becoming the coloniser. But this movement away from their first adopted country was also embedded in the violence of racial repression and the uncertainties of predicted social chaos.

My aunt told me everything that she knew about the Twofold Tamil Rule, mixed with a good dose of stories of ghosts and African elves used by magicians to perform their great mysteries. In fact, the Rule was of less interest to me than the appealing idea of trapping one of these elves to help my faltering career as a part-time performer of magical illusions. She gave full instructions for its capture; that the very seeing of an elf was enough to make it your slave, provided it saw you seeing it. But the complexities of being in a rural African locale, at the precise moment of dusk when an elf might be seen riding on one of the cattle, waving a small herding stick, was too much to accomplish. So I turned to testing the Twofold Tamil Rule.

Before my return from England, riding a bus through Shepherd's Bush (no doubt filled with accountants), I suddenly spotted a smartly outfitted shop: Tommy N. Childs – Electronics. And as the red double-decker London bus slowly plodded its way through the traffic, I saw the unmistakeable Tommy Narayadu sitting earnestly behind a repair desk. Tommy knows his Tamil, I thought, and a fictional character from a V.S. Naipaul novel suddenly came to life.

೫

Upon my return from England, in fulfilment of my promise to my father, I told my brother everything that was said to me. Ever the sceptic, he wanted proof, and we waited for an opportune moment to use the Rule. In the oppressive political conditions of the time, there would be ample opportunity.

In our case, it would never be against the obvious oppressors, but those who had caught their own elves and were skilled at presenting the most believable facades of liberal conduct. Our first victim was the editor of *The Weekly Digest*, William Neary.

Neary became editor when his popular predecessor suddenly died. There were rumours that he had been poisoned by the security branch for his outspoken editorials against the oppressive racist regime. Neary got the job more because of seniority than actual political commitment to the liberation of the country. He was not even a wishy-washy liberal. He was a colonial through and through, and if he had any antagonism towards the Afrikaner government, it was because of the old English-Afrikaner feud rather than any sympathy for black political aspirations. If he did suggest as much, then it was just a role that he adopted for the occasion.

Just out of university, with a degree cum laude in English, I spotted a *Weekly Digest* advertisement for a sub-editor. The newspaper, under Neary's predecessor, employed one Indian and a few black journalists, most of whom were trained on the job with nothing but pure talent. I reckoned I had both the talent and the qualifications. I applied, certain of success. The many journalists that I knew on the paper supported my application, but Neary would have nothing of it.

'He's a raving Marxist,' he said to Emmanuel, the Indian journalist at the time. Apparently Neary had attended an uncommon multi-racial youth meeting, where he encountered my rather outspoken younger brother, and he confused him with me. But what if I were a Marxist, what did that have to do with the job of sub-editing? Did he think that I would insert Marxist maxims in the by-lines, or distort copy to reflect a Marxist perspective? So I sent William Neary a stinging letter, which almost cost Emmanuel his job. I was sorry that I had implicated him, but I wasn't sorry that I had sent the letter. This was a perfect opportunity to test the Twofold Tamil Rule.

No skittles appeared to me, no violent emotion, just a verbal gesture accompanied by, 'Let's give him the Twofold Tamil Rule.'

Now, unbeknown to Neary, his extra-marital activities with a certain widow were being monitored by the security branch, just in case they needed to bring him in line. But a day after we effected the Rule, the ruling party's recruitment office was discreetly informed that Neary was game for joining, a major scoop in a city that mainly voted for the English party of the time. And the address given to the recruiting officer was that of the widow's home with instructions to pay a call at about nine that night.

Neary and the dear widow were just about to con-summate their bi-weekly alliance when the doorbell rang. Caught totally off guard by this late visit, Neary rushed to the door to see who it was, in quite a state of dishevelment.

'We're recruiting new members,' the officer said

to the harried Neary, 'and we would really like you to join. All we need is your signature, sir.'

Neary, consumed with thoughts of another kind of joining, and now on a deadline to meet his regular departure at ten, never bothered to check what he was being asked to join, but simply signed and immediately got rid of the recruitment officer. And that was the end of Neary.

Every newspaper was leaked the scoop that William Neary had joined the ruling party – his signature on the enrolment form prominently printed for all to see. Neary couldn't even scream 'framed'; they had him cornered. Before long, Neary resigned, and *The Weekly Digest* once more became a newspaper of integrity. And in an ironic way, the security branch had aided the whole affair which left them with sulphurous egg on their face. The Twofold Tamil Rule had struck twice.

⌘

Every culture has its orthodoxies and taboos. For much of our early modern history our kings and priests forbade any questioning of their authority; the taboo would be logically constructed around an emotional centre, and in the centre of that centre would be the need for power and fear of the unknown, like a needle-thin spike piercing the pupils of our eyes, making us blind. And this holds true even now. In Orwell's *Animal Farm*, the pigs are above reproach, even as they start to resemble the humans, because, the logic holds, they were once part of the oppressed animals. When this happens, sentiment masks the obvious: the grasping for power – which is really a fleeing from fear, but wonderfully packaged, because the packaging, to keep and increase the power, plays on other subsidiary fears. And when we believe this story, we lose something vital. We lose the ability to truly articulate the dishonesty that pervades the Emperor and his courtiers, and his illusion of new clothes. In the illusion of our freedom, we become even more fearful, such that only a child's mind, as in the fable, can shatter the deception.

The years of the struggle had its own taboos among those in the struggle; although some were not really in the struggle, they just looked like they were. This was so with Jimmy Hertzog, a comrade who was hard to define racially. He was most probably classed 'coloured', but he certainly had some Indian in him, and God knows where the Afrikaner surname came from. But as they say in modern parlance, he was smooth, and he played the white liberals like a classical guitar.

He used the liberals at home for the protection they afforded him; it was the liberals in the western countries whom he relieved of their money as they cried about the atrocities of apartheid. My father would have called those 'crocodile tears'. And he spoke the radical talk so well. In five minutes you were ashamed to be eating a decent meal or driving a nice car. Now he's probably into some big black empowerment scheme, bleeding dry the same kinds of people. And maybe they deserve it.

Back in the height of the struggle, Jimmy played his role with aplomb, but ever so often threatening to go out of character and actually join the struggle in the deprivation of London or the desert of New York. Until you realised that the gesture was part of the role.

In the most bizarre, surreal way, Jimmy created a small empire that stretched throughout the land; he created alternative Centres of Poetic Justice – centres for black literary development – for the disadvantaged that had a most wonderful vision in the face of the oppressions that were so rife. But because Jimmy was not straight, neither were his centres. Each one was flawed by deceptions that hid the truth in eloquent reports. Of course, it's also not true that nothing was accomplished, but what was achieved paled in comparison with what could have been achieved. However, when you operate with bleeding heart liberals within an oppressive social order, it becomes so easy to evoke the taboo of questioning. So, no one questioned Jimmy or his impressively produced reports, nor did Jimmy really want to question his regional co-ordinators. One was using the Centre's resources to develop grand-sounding solar houses for the poor, but with a technology that resembled the Emperor's new clothes; another operated a wonderful rural arts development scheme, but kept most of the profits for herself; and yet another held social gatherings for affluent white and Indian youth – with some coloureds and blacks thrown in – and then wrote lyrical reports of racial unity which became another kind of poetic truth. No one mentioned that for the few Indians it was just a wonderful opportunity to meet white and black girls; and for the whites it was time to relieve their conscience for being so wealthy, or to play politics, safely. It's also true that there were the few that went beyond playing, but they would have done so anyway.

My contact with Jimmy occurred when he had read one of my poems in an alternative magazine for black literature. He wrote to me saying that he wanted to meet when next he was visiting his Centre in the city.

When we did meet it was all about him and the Centres and how I was prostituting myself and the struggle with the kinds of apolitical pieces I was writing. And if one looked at it objectively, without context, he may have been correct about the poems that were published. I was duly chastised, and about to pledge allegiance to poems about the rape of Mother Africa, when he came up close to me and said:

'So I believe the white chicks are really game here. Can you organise?'

I was dumbfounded and became an incoherent idiot, muttering something about my constitutional inability with girls, when he said he wanted to spend some time at the beach. And he left, in his hired car, taking some bottles of wine with him. All my life I had someone delude me with their stories of what was true; whether it was the damnation of eating steak and kidney pies (I once hid a chicken pie under my bed when a staunch Hindu paid an unannounced visit during suppertime, thinking, in my childish fear, that pies were the problem), the threat of malevolent spirits entering our house if we came home after midnight, or the fanatical religious Witness in Clarke's End scaring the hell out of us with his stories of the end of the world and Armageddon, which was going to happen precisely at the beginning of 1975 – his wife almost cut off his watchtower when she awoke to his affair with a fellow Witness. And now I was being told what to write. I evoked the Rule; it had nothing to do with girls or wine, but the hypocrisy of it all.

The next morning Jimmy was found, still fairly inebriated, in a ditch, the hired car smashed up quite badly. Poetic justice. He had an unknown young woman with him, no doubt a comrade who needed a lift. And Jimmy's smashed-up car would just be another expense that some donor had paid for. During the struggle and after, donors would pay for many smashed cars, none of them smashed in any act of war, but because the drivers were smashed; a kind of perverted symbol of being politically active.

'You smashed a car? Good. We've got a job for you and a thousand shares in a company that's going to make millions selling renewable bicycle licences. If you smashed two cars you get two thousand shares, but you can't get two jobs. But we're looking into that.'

Jimmy went into a kind of seclusion after the incident. He disbanded the Centres, liquidated the assets and disappeared. Maybe he finally went into exile, I don't know; but with a cynicism that I find hard to shake, I half expect to see him in the financial section of the newspaper, making a big corporate deal that will benefit the country's disadvantaged. I believe the first half of my prediction; the second half has yet to take form with the many others who are too dishonest to say: 'Look, I'm a self-centred business-man/woman, and I want to make as much money for myself as I can. After all, I was oppressed, so now is the opportunity that history has given me.' Without any moral judgement appended to that statement, we would have to at least call it honest.

ଔ

My brother and I continued to encounter many variations of Jimmy Hertzog, and each received the Twofold Tamil Rule when the situation required it. In fact, it's as if the situation used the Rule rather than it being used through our wilful volition.

And the Rule worked mysteriously. A high-handed, self-righteous principal of a university located in a particularly oppressive ethnic homeland, and protected by the might of its security forces, was brought down by a blow to the centre when the puppet government collapsed taking the principal with it; my brother's insufferable head of department suddenly developed acute inflammation of the knees which rendered him unavailable for a meeting that decided my brother's tenure. The head of department, in this American university, was Indian and part of the new wave of Indian immigrants to America, and he felt irrationally threatened by another Indian's presence, although frequently he would ask my brother: 'Know any good business opportunities for the sideline? Academics' salary not good enough for all the people back home.'

Fortunately, in his place of birth in India, the fame of Two-Hit Pillai was either unknown, or had been forgotten. He might have made the connection. My brother, a medical scientist, successfully treated the painful knees with some of our aunt Ambika's herbal remedies, but kept the ingredients a secret in case the stricken colleague got ideas to increase his university salary with a herbal shop on the side. If that happened, more than his knees would have been inflamed. He would have received from my brother, in my father's words, 'two kicks up the backside.'

Five

When I first saw the Principal, she was still the Principal-Elect, having just been given the top post to lead the Institute of Research, but only to assume office in the new year. And she cut a rather lonely figure amidst a sea of racial others at a function to honour the end of the selection process. I felt, irrationally, sorry for her.

80

She would have a tough task, I thought, to lead the Institute into a new era, with its history of tensions riding waves of so many competing interests and ideologies. But she could make a difference, from the little I had heard about her. I was wrong.

On her first day of office, I sent a welcome package of publications from the Publications Unit that I headed, hoping that at some point the Principal would pay a visit to the Publications Office and give support. That never ever happened. Too busy, I thought. But no other form of acknowledgement, either.

Perhaps rigorous academic publications frightened the Principal; her impressive list of publications that graced her inauguration programme were actually quarterly reports that she had filed as head of the very small department of Collective Dementia in a very small community college in England, where she apparently lived in exile, if exile is the right word. But these were minor initial suspicions; surely she was appointed for actual or perceived leadership qualities?

The Institute should have known better. Its history of appointing researchers from the field of Dementia as administrators never paid the dividends in wisdom that we erroneously assigned to them. And that's because the field of Dementia itself is a grand schizophrenic illusion that is uncertain of itself as it muddles along in its attempt to be scientific about its inquiries that actually have their origins in areas of human belief that are no different to my Aunt Ambika's ghosts.

And while we waited for the leader to emerge, the leader was planning her ostentatious inauguration to mark her occupation of office, which, incidentally, she redecorated in a garish pink. After the event, attended by the country's dignitaries, she was heard to refer to the inauguration as her 'coronation'. Surely, the wrong word, someone pointed out.

'No,' she said, 'I'm of royal blood.'

The revolution was over, and the aristocracy was taking control. In my grandfather's worldview, she was not a Pillai, someone who had earned her position, but a pretender.

After the inauguration, and the promise of research utopia, schemes were being hatched in the Manor House, and Napoleon was on the march. And like the famous novel about the perversion of power, there suddenly appeared Napoleon's aides, Sonic Boom and Pleaser.

Sonic Boom was the name for a large, booming union man who came from one of the administration departments overseeing research output. Long given to the politics of the Institute, he presented himself as a revolutionary of the highest order, except that his only contact with the actual struggle was that he once thought about taking an active part in it. He wasn't even close to Jimmy Hertzog, who looked like Che Guevara next to Sonic Boom. Pretenders make the best henchmen, because they need the favours of the dictator to get someplace else. Sonic Boom became the Principal's chief articulator in the two-man (except one was a woman) committee, the Commission for Research Control (CRC).

The other aide was Pleaser. If Big Mouth played the bad cop, then it was Pleaser who played the good cop. With her low-pitched, sultry voice, the duo made a kind of vocal Laurel and Hardy. And the Principal got her from the Unit of Chronic Dementia, a kind of comrade in arms. Pleaser also saw herself as a rebel, even though her rebellion may have been on a small domestic scale, like smoking the odd joint, and she may have looked at pictures of the struggle.

With Sonic Boom and Pleaser in place, the Principal set up a few defining meetings for the Institute that showed that our research output was way below target, which had implications for future funding and the very existence of the institution, we were told. We were being made to believe a story, carefully orchestrated to resemble some truth, defined by Sonic Boom's facts and Pleaser's figures (her own figure was far from pleasing). The same kind of story-making that the United States used to invade Iraq. I call it the lizard effect.

The lizard effect has been suggested by a conspiracy theorist who claims that most of the world's most powerful leaders are actually alien lizards in the guise of human beings. That sounds far-fetched, but actually it's closer to home than we think, if we see that power activates something in our reptilian brains, so much so that we start to behave in ways, which, upon reflection in the stillness of approaching death, we may look upon in total horror as to how this madness came about.

Lizards and pigs mess up metaphoric continuity, but what the hell, in reality, on the farm, the pigs were actually lizards.

Then came the CRC's ultimate weapon – FUQA (pronounced 'fukwa'), which stood for Forensic Unit Qualifying Audit. They say that there are no slips of the tongue, that unintended meanings are actually intended by the sub-conscious. If this is the case then there was a subliminal intention behind an acronym that could have been created in a more logical way. No, I believe that we were being told, blatantly, that we were FUQA'd.

FUQA's job – really the job of Sonic Boom and Pleaser – was to determine which research units were profitable, and which were not, and all along I believed that the Publications Unit, serving the Arts, was safe. I was wrong. The Arts, especially, was being targeted, notwithstanding the fact that the researchers in various Units of the Arts were recognised nationally and internationally for their professional endeavours. We were naïve to think that the Arts was going to be supported by administrators from Dementia; the one research discipline is fully aware of its role in society, the other is an outgrowth of society's schizophrenic face. Artists are never going to be recognised by the demented.

Now, through all this manic activity, when certain researchers and their disciplines were basically spat upon by Sonic Boom and Pleaser, the Principal suddenly disappeared from the running of the Institute. The CRC had taken control, while she took up numerous paid positions in numerous nationwide bodies of so-called national interest. (Many years later she would deny that she received any salary for such services rendered, but conceded that she had received honoraria, payments which actually totalled more than her grossly overpaid annual salary.) And in these bodies, all targeted for re-organisation, she set up similar versions of the CRC. The Principal was like a destructive anti-viral medication, killing both good and bad cells, which she saw as a cleansing. No doubt she wanted only the royal blood flowing.

ଓ

The Twofold Tamil Rule, strangely, was silent. It could not be evoked, coerced... nothing. And when, at an important meeting, the Principal finally emerged, placating the troubled about the insecurities of their livelihood, I felt that there may be an obvious reason why the Rule was not working, we were not going to lose our jobs.

85

'It's not the intention of me or the CRC to take away your jobs,' she said in her high-pitched voice with its strong English accent still very evident (what irony, we were again being colonised by the English). 'We are simply doing long overdue audits that will determine the best way to reorganise our research potential. Researchers from affected Units will be absorbed elsewhere.'

But obviously the Principal's phrase 'reorganise our research potential' meant something entirely different to her than it meant to us. Shortly afterwards, when we got the unexpected letter from the Principal informing us of the termination of our posts, with one month to leave the Institute, it became obvious that the Principal's phrase meant 'I am a liar, so sue me.'

And there was something about the Principal that bothered me, but at the time it was just a nagging feeling of something perceived but yet unrecognised. Later it would come to me; she looked remarkably like the first Principal of the Institute, made head by the old apartheid regime. Did she always have that resemblance, I wondered? To confuse matters, the first head was a man.

The Principal's timing was perfect: Our exit, for almost fifty of us, would take place during the December summer vacation. The Institute would start the New Year cleansed.

☙

Obsession is a kind of madness, and I became obsessed. Like an old curse resurfacing, I knew in my very being what my grandfather and father had gone through; my grandfather when he was cornered by Williamson, and my father when he was made impotent by the fakir. Here was I, repeating the pattern of impotence at a most crucial time. Some Rule!

My obsessions ranged from elaborate plans to scare the wits out of the Principal and her deadly duo – Sonic Boom and Pleaser – through convincing letters and/or objects of witchcraft that threatened their safety, to absolutely ridiculous ideas like puncturing their tyres.

But that is the nature of thought. It is seized by a story, and then plays out infinite versions of it, and all through this the pain continues unabated. And it does this because thought is really a phantom, one of my Aunt Ambika's ghosts, which is only made real in the believing. But when thought is on the rampage, the madness cannot be pierced, unless life itself intervenes.

And life did. That December, shortly before Christmas, we experienced unseasonable torrential rains, which caused major flooding within a matter of hours. Coming down the stairs of our car port to the patio below, my arms full of breakfast foods for our holiday guests, my brother and his family, I slipped and bounced down the stairs like a ball. It's as if life gave me two kicks up the backside, and that part of my anatomy, when I managed painfully to look at it in the mirror, was a deep purple, like a grotesque-looking aubergine. The streams of history, it appeared, converged at this unlikely place.

Confined to my bed with a fever that accompanied the pain, the racing, screaming thoughts about the Principal and Sonic Boom and Pleaser became even more insistent. Whole movies, with me as the hero obtaining revenge, played one after the other, each movie a distinct variation of the previous one. Perhaps I would need to seek assistance from those who researched chronic dementia, I reluctantly conceded to myself. Then the pain and the fever overwhelmed the movies, and I subsided into an uneasy sleep.

When I awoke the fever was gone, and the pain was now a dull throb. I went to the bathroom, and in the mirror I instantly perceived what had become of my grandfather more than eighty years before. And I knew with a visceral certainty what he had said in his Indian English.

'Meera, Meera, look what I've become.'

I crumpled to the floor in a desperate grief, but unlike my grandfather, I did not die.

Epilogue

My brother said that when he found me I was an incoherent, blathering idiot.

'You were going on about pigs and lizards and Napoleon. I would have said it was the effects of concussion, but you didn't fall on your head, unless that's where your brains are.'

'What else did I say?' I asked, wanting to make sense of the senseless.

'You said that the pigs started to change because they didn't know that the lizards in the farmers were also in them. Sounds like you were concocting a science fiction story that got to you.'

೧೩

The Twofold Tamil Rule was never ever dormant; it had finally found its full expression. And that expression is the direct recognition that the other and I are made of the same stuff. Napoleon's destiny was to become like Jones; he could not do otherwise while the lizard reigned. And the lizard reigns, it seems, when we deny that it exists. A paradox. But to deny this is to bring back the ghosts and the terror of their presence, which is really the terror of a lie made real.

Mature human beings, if history is correct, seem to know a lot about lizards. They just call it another name. One such human being, by the name of Nelson Rolihlahla Mandela once said: 'As we are liberated from our own fear, our presence automatically liberates others.'

delusion

Imagining John Lennon

I
Double Fantasy

'So, you're not John Lennon?' she asks.

'No,' I reply, 'I only appear to be. I admit it's a good likeness, but it's just a show, and...' And I pause, trying to see if I can be as accurate as I possibly can.

'Yes?'

'And I have no clue about how it happened. How I came to be John Lennon, I mean. But I'm not. I never was.'

My thoughts characterise her as earnest and well-meaning, with clothes to show herself off as voluptuous. Beyond that, there is just silence. I am not even waiting for her next remark, or curious about the possible direction and consequences of this interview. I just sit.

It is an interview, I'm aware, to figure me out. Ever since I announced to family and friends that

I'm not John Lennon, it's been something like this. Questions. Many, many questions. And I understand their difficulty, even their fear, so I try to answer as best I can.

Yes, I know I have the John Lennon face and haircut, and the John Lennon glasses, but surely they must have had their suspicions, when I have only a picture of Yoko in my wallet? No actual Yoko anywhere. I have always asked them about that. But they evaded or seemed nonplussed by that question and similar insistent questions when my sense of not being John Lennon started to surface. It's like they needed me to be John Lennon, rather than being unequivocally convinced that I was. So, somehow, they would convince me of my John Lennon-ness, and I, not quite certain myself, would run the whole thing again. After all, I was *John Lennon*, so why not?

But she knows all this. When they brought me here they described my periodic confusions, but this time I thought I had them cornered. I had proof. But that only made matters worse. Their response was almost instant, and angry. Very angry. I had to be set right; I had to be disabused of this notion that I wasn't who I have always been. It was important for me, they said. But their eyes told another truth, like her eyes before me now.

'I'm told that you have some kind of evidence that you're not, and never were, John Lennon. Conclusive proof.'

'Yes,' I reply. And from my shirt pocket I take out

94

the carefully folded printout of an article. I pass it to her, and she reads aloud.

'In the late afternoon of 8 December 1980, in New York City, Mark David Chapman met Lennon as he left his home in the Dakota building for a recording session and got his copy of *Double Fantasy* autographed. This goodwill gesture of Lennon signing an album for a presumed fan was caught by a photographer present, and would be published on the front page of the New York Daily News later that week. Chapman remained in the vicinity of the Dakota building for most of the day as a fireworks demonstration in nearby Central Park distracted the doorman and passers-by.

Later that evening, Lennon and Ono returned to their apartment from recording Ono's single "Walking on Thin Ice" for their next album. At 10.50pm, their limousine pulled up to the entrance of the Dakota. Ono got out of the car first, followed by Lennon. As Ono went in, Lennon glanced at Chapman, then proceeded on through the entrance to the building.

As Lennon walked past him, Chapman calmly called out "Mr. Lennon?" As Lennon turned, Chapman crouched into what witnesses called a "combat" stance and fired five hollow point bullets. One bullet missed, but four bullets entered Lennon's back and shoulder. One of the four bullets fatally pierced his aorta.'

If there was ever an example of controlled terror, it's what I see now. It's not so much in what she says as in how the whole body contracts, and how little nervous mannerisms appear, like the slight tapping of the right forefinger on the desk. Like a school teacher about to chew your head off for a very bad piece of work. With her it also expresses her certainty of knowledge, knowledge which she is no doubt going to use to disprove my case.

'And this came from where?' she asks. I detect a slight disdain in her voice.

'Wikipedia,' I reply.

'Ah, Wikipedia,' she says, almost triumphant. 'Wikipedia, that fount of unconfirmed information on the internet. This makes matters so much clearer.'

'Unconfirmed?' I ask.

'Yes, information from dubious sources made plausible at times by the indiscriminate mixture of fact and fiction.' She speaks these words with effortless authority and academic certainty.

'So, John Lennon is not dead?'

'No.'

'But how can you be certain?' I ask.

And she looks at me with what must surely be eyes of relief posing as something else. Perhaps eyes that want to make me feel safe and secure.

'Because *you're* John Lennon. You've never been anyone but John Lennon. Everyone knows that. *You* know that.'

'And Yoko?' I ask. 'Where is she? And where is my...' But she interrupts me before I can continue, as if to control this delusion once and for all.

'We all know who you are. *You* know who you are. This avoidance of what's so obvious is what we have to address. But, out of curiosity, if you're not John Lennon, who *are* you?'

'I don't know, and the truth is, it doesn't matter. Not in the least. Not in the least.' As I say this, a flash of something dark crosses her face. But quickly the habit of control is there, erasing all traces of any disturbance.

'But that's the point, it does matter! You can't really live not knowing who you are, or denying what you've always been. After all, *you're* John Lennon. We'll find ways to bring you back to yourself. There's nothing to worry about.'

'You're right, there's nothing to worry about,' I say quietly.

She smiles benignly at me when I say these words, but she doesn't question whether we mean the same thing.

She arranges her posture in a way that tells me that our time is over. As she does, I catch her name badge set against the breast pocket of her white coat.

'You're Dr...' I am about to say.

'Spears,' she replies. 'Britney Spears.'

II
Blow Out The man

The soulful humming of the mid-sixties hit, *When a Man Loves a Woman*, tells me that my orderly is about to enter my room with my morning tea. That's his signature tune.

'Good morning John,' he says cheerfully. And then, teasingly, 'Oh, I forgot, you're not John, you're…?'

'You,' I reply.

'Me?' he asks incredulously. 'Man, you're going to be here a long time. A long, long, long time. What a pity, with all that talent. Now tell me, how are *you* me?' he asks as he sets the tray of tea and biscuits on the little table next to my bed.

'I can't,' I reply. 'Not in any way that would make sense. You would have to see for yourself, you would have to be there.'

'That's no good John. I mean you can't go around speaking these crazy things and expect people to believe you. You're throwing your life away. It will be finished, any day now. Give it up, man, give it up.'

'That's not possible,' I reply, taking a sip of the hot, sweet tea. 'You can't give up what you really are, you just can't. I can't be stopped.'

He stands still, and looks at me intently; but not as if in deep thought, but as if in the absence of thought.

'You know, I kinda like you. There's something quiet about you, like you're here, but not here. Know what I mean? Oh, hell, I'm talking crazy just like you.'

'Yes,' I laugh, 'it's kind of infectious.'

'You mean I'm going to become like you. No way, man, I like being Percy.'

'I know,' I reply. 'We all like being who we think we are until the lie just doesn't hold anymore. When the pain gets too much. So, you're Percy Sledge, the great soul singer?' Percy looks at me like I've uttered the worst blasphemy.

'Man, what a thing to ask! Everyone here knows who I am. I'm Percy Sledge, the King of Soul. That's who I am.'

'Then what,' I ask politely, 'are you doing here? Why aren't you outside this place, doing your thing, singing your songs?'

'To take care of crazies, like you,' he replies, like I missed the most obvious of reasons.

'True,' I reply, 'but that doesn't tell me why *you*, Percy Sledge, are doing this work? You're not doing this as some kind of part-time community service, are you? You're here, full-time, right?'

'Yeah, I'm here full-time. You know that,' he responds, but his voice seems uncertain about something, and there's a long pause. 'Yeah, I'm here full-time,' and then there's a sudden stop, as if caused by some deep recognition, and he begins to cry. 'Oh, God, I'm getting crazy like you.'

'Come, Percy, you're too pretty to cry,' I say gently, paraphrasing a song I remember from somewhere.

'Hey, man, that's one of mine,' he says, his face lighting up when he hears the words. He wipes his eyes with a spotless, white handkerchief. 'She's too pretty to cry,' he says, giving the correct title of the song. And then, half pleading, 'Help me. What am I really living for?'

'Percy, like John, doesn't really exist, so there's no one to help, and life's doing the living anyway. But we can stop the world tonight,' I say, playing on

Sledge's famous song titles, 'because that's the way I live my life. Push Mr Pride aside, Percy, that's my special prayer. This isn't about self-preservation, or warm and tender love. This will tear you up, and it can't be stopped. Percy,' I say emphatically, 'nothing comes to a sleeper but a dream.'

'What I don't know…' begins Percy, but I interrupt.

'You'll never know, Percy, never, but you'll have the heart of a child. You've got that something wonderful, we all have, but we just can't *know* it. So we go looking for it in being what we're not. And that something wonderful becomes our tears. That's the fear that drives us, that makes life seem just out of reach.'

'It seems all wrong but it's alright,' he says, starting to smile. 'It's hard to believe, but now I'm talking crazy like you, and it feels faithful and true.'

'This seeing, it comes like a thief in the night, it comes softly to you. Most of those love songs, sweet and pretty and all, just don't cut it. About real love, the good love, I mean. Not "true love travels on a gravel road" and all that nonsense.'

Percy is now all lit up, as if walking in the sun and seeing from a different place; as if standing on a mountain.

'You mean love is where life begins?' he asks.

'Yes, something like that. You can always get it where you got it. Which is right here, right now.'

'I always believed yesterday was a better day. Or tomorrow will be.'

'We all did. But there's no time; there's no yesterday or tomorrow but what we think. *That's* the real craziness. See this, see this now, and then you won't need any help to make it through the night.'

'Is that…?'

'Yes. That's the way I live my life. It's unchanging love.'

'How do you know…?' he asks, but pauses, as if trying to frame the right question. I complete the question for him because it's evident where he's going.

'How do you know for certain, absolutely, that you're really not Percy?'

Percy nods. I continue.

'It's like when you know when a boy becomes a man. You just know.'

'I think I understand,' he says. Tears flow again, but this time they glisten against a radiant face.

Percy is about to say something else, when there's an announcement over the intercom.

'Percy Sledge, Percy Sledge, please contact reception. You're wanted.'

It's the receptionist calling for Percy.

'I have to go; I've been here too long. But hey, in crazy talk, no time has actually passed, has it?'

I nod in agreement.

'So, so long,' he says as he walks out slowly.

'Remember, you've got that something wonderful. No, you *are* that something wonderful. It's everything you'll ever need.'

'If this is the last time…' he begins to say.

'If this is the last time that I'll see you as Percy?'

'Yes.'

'Nothing will have changed. And everything will. And that warm and tender love thing, it still goes on, but without too many rivers to cross. It doesn't blow out the man. You'll see. You will. And it will keep you faithful and true.'

'Thank you, John. I mean...'

'John's alright. It's been kinda fun playing him. And Percy, there's no one to thank when one brings it on home. But gratitude will follow you like the aroma of sugar pudding.'

As Percy leaves, another announcement calls for him.

'Percy Sledge, Percy Sledge, please see Dr Presley immediately.'

III
What You Get Is What You See

Tina explodes into my room.

'Percy-less, Percy-less, what kind of name is Percy-less?' she asks, almost shouting, standing with her hands on her generous hips, her bosom heaving with agitation.

'Well, it's definitely not Percy-full,' I reply. 'Get it? Percival ... Percy-full?'

'He's Percy-fool, alright, Percy-fool,' she exclaims indignantly, 'and you, Mr John Lennon, are responsible. Getting that good man to change his name, getting him to be crazy like you.'

Tina is not one of the staff. Like me, she's an inmate, but unlike me she's not here for anything considered too threatening. She's here, voluntarily, for substance abuse.

'I know what this is about,' she says, starting to pace slowly in front of my bed, using exaggerated hand movements to punctuate her remarks. Like most of the black women on TV. In fact, that's what I'm watching, a character from a TV show, and the name of the show doesn't matter. But this is not something I will tell her, in the mood she's in.

'This is about white folk making black people crazy,' she says emphatically. 'This is some kinda plot to stop us black people from being who we are. You're some kind of undercover agent.'

I can easily point out the contradictions in Tina's accusations, but I know they won't mean anything to her. She's fully caught up in her story. So, I just listen. That's what I find myself doing these days, just listening.

'We've had a hard time to make it in this world. But what do you do to us, the Michael Jacksons, the O J Simpsons, the Richard Priors...? You try to bring us down, to make us the nobodies that you want us to be. Taking our names away. Goddam-right-wing-George Bush-keep-the-country-white nonsense.'

'You're right, Tina, it is nonsense,' I say. Tina finally stops her pacing and looks suspiciously at me.

'You're right, there is a conspiracy to keep us down, but it's not a black or white thing, it's the way of the world. It's not a conspiracy created by any one group of people, although it may show up in what people do to each other. It's a conspiracy within our thinking; believing the stories we tell each other and ourselves.'

'You're not fooling me with that kinda talk,' she says quickly. 'The doctors, they've told me what you're saying, how you can mess with people's minds.'

I want to emphasise the point that it's our minds messing with us, but I let it be.

'Look at poor Percy, he's not himself. Talking crazy all the time. Using his songs in every sentence.'

'Saying what, Tina?'

'Saying there's no "me". What's that supposed to mean if not to make us crazy? I'm me, period.'

'Which me? Which period? The young girl? The lover? The mother…?'

'That's all of me,' she says forcefully, certain of herself.

'Yes, they are, but only in the stories we remember and tell. What are you *now*, in this moment?'

Tina doesn't reply. But I suspect it's because she is still in her story of who she thinks she is. Not because she's really looking. I try again.

'Tina, turnaround.'

'Tina Turner,' she snaps.

'Yes, I know, but I meant "turnaround". Turn your attention away from what you're looking at to what's doing the looking. That's the real "you".'

'Get away, fool. That's what got Percy all messed up. You're not doing that to me. I'm getting outta here.'

She's almost at the door when I say to her, 'What you get is what you see. What you see is not a story. You could say it's love, *you're* love.'

'What's love got to do with it?' she asks, almost sarcastically, and leaves.

'Everything,' I find myself saying, but there's no one to hear.

IV
Let It Be

They've finally let me go. Exasperated, I suppose. But I've enjoyed myself, although Tina yelling at me whenever she could was getting a bit too much. Not so much for me personally, but for the others. But it didn't seem to touch Percy at all. He is just pure radiance.

I'm walking back to my apartment, when I see a shadowy figure. A face that I remember from somewhere.

As I walk past him, he calls out, 'Mr. Lennon?' I hardly have time to respond when he crouches, pointing something at me...

In an instant there is absolute certainty of who I am as all pretence dissolves forever. Ah, those words of wisdom...Let It Be.

Notes

Percy Sledge songs referred to:
Any day now
Blow out the man
Come softly to me
Everything you'll ever need
Faithful and true
Hard to believe
Heart of a child
Help me
Help me make it through the night
I can't be stopped
If this is the last time
It tears me up
It's all wrong but it's alright
Just out of reach
Love is where life begins
My special prayer
Nothing comes to a sleeper but a dream
Push Mr Pride aside
Self preservation
She's too pretty to cry
Standing on the mountain
Stop the world tonight
Sudden stop
Sugar pudding
That's the way I live my life
The good love

Thief in the night
Time
Too many rivers to cross
True love travels on a gravel road
Unchanging love
Wanted
Warm and tender love
What am I living for
What I don't know
When a boy becomes a man
When a man loves a woman
Yesterday was a better day
You can always get it where you got it
You had to be there
You've got that something wonderful

Tina Turner songs referred to:
Undercover agent for the blues
Way of the world
What you get is what you see
What's love got to do with it?

John Lennon song referred to:
Let It Be